THIS BOOK
BELONGS TO

_____

_____

Daily Strength for Women

A 365-DAY DEVOTIONAL

BroadStreet
PUBLISHING

BroadStreet Publishing Group, LLC.
Savage, Minnesota, USA
Broadstreetpublishing.com

Daily Strength for Women

978-1-4245-6105-6
978-1-4245-6106-3 (eBook)

Design by Chris Garborg | garborgdesign.com
Compiled and edited by Michelle Winger | literallyprecise.com

Printed in China.

20 21 22 23 24 25 26   7 6 5 4 3 2 1

The LORD is my
strength and shield.
I trust him with
all my heart.
He helps me, and my
heart is filled with joy.
I burst out in songs
of thanksgiving.

Psalm 28:8 nlt

Intro

You can walk in confidence when you rely on God to be your strength. Be encouraged with truth as you spend time with God, reflecting on these devotions, Scriptures, and prayers. As you spend time with him, he will fill you with peace and hope for each day.

Let your heavenly Father show you that, through him, even in your weakest moments, you are radiant and you are strong. Take courage in God's love for you and be ready to conquer each day!

January

God is our refuge and strength,
an ever-present help in trouble.

PSALM 46:1 NIV

Book of Life

Your eyes beheld my unformed substance.
In your book were written
all the days that were formed for me,
when none of them as yet existed.

PSALM 139:16 NRSV

It's the day of new beginnings and you might be feeling a mixture of emotions. There is bound to be excitement about the possibilities that are waiting just around the corner, but there also might be overwhelming thoughts about the trials that could lie ahead or fear of the unknown.

Whatever your thoughts and feelings are about this day, remember that you have the spirit of Christ in your heart and mind, ready to help you in all of your decisions and strengthening you through any challenges. Head into this day with the confidence that he created you and already knows who you are, and who you are going to become!

What do you need courage to take on this year with grace and skill, knowing that God is right there with you?

Feeling Stuck

The Sovereign LORD is my strength!
He makes me as surefooted as a deer,
able to tread upon the heights.

HABAKKUK 3:19 NLT

"Local authorities are reporting blizzard conditions on the Interstate…" Did your pulse just quicken, your muscles tense? No one likes to feel stuck, and blinding snow and unmoving vehicles on every side can cause even the most rational, laid-back woman to imagine leaping from her car and running over rooftops and across hoods, action hero style. What a fun way to test out the traction on your new winter boots. Or not. Anyway, stuck is stuck, right?

Maybe we feel stuck in our everyday lives. A job that doesn't utilize our gifts, a relationship that's more take than give, a habit that's edging toward addiction. Unlike that snow-covered freeway-turned-parking-lot, there is a direction to turn when circumstances have you feeling boxed in. Turn your face toward the Lord; let him fill you with the strength to move.

*Where are you stuck right now? Professionally, personally,
or perhaps in your prayer life, is there an area
where you've simply stopped moving?*

Body Parts

Just as each of us has one body with many members,
and these members do not all have the same function,
so in Christ we, though many, form one body,
and each member belongs to all the others.

ROMANS 12:4-5 NIV

A tooth is such a small part of the body, but when it begins to ache, it can be debilitating! The human body is fascinating in this way. God has created all of our parts to be distinct yet interdependent.

As a Christian, you are part of the body of Christ. More important than trying to distinguish which part you are is the recognition of just how important your unique gifts are to the health of the whole body. You were created to belong to something that is greater than yourself. The Bible acknowledges that God has given us different gifts that are not for our individual gain. God designed our gifts to be used in harmony with others' gifts.

Will you allow God to speak to you today about how you can use your gifts for the good of the entire body of Christ?

Comfort and Strength

May our Lord Jesus Christ himself and God our Father,
who loved us and by his grace gave us eternal comfort and a wonderful
hope, comfort you and strengthen you in every good thing you do and say.

2 THESSALONIANS 2:16-17 NLT

After being confused about when the Lord Jesus would return, and after facing extreme persecution, the Thessalonians needed the Lord's refreshing hope, comfort, and strength. By God's grace, they were able to face every obstacle with confidence and strength. In every action and every word, they were able to choose to do good. Nothing was too much for them because God had demonstrated his love to them.

We also can face all things and cling to what is good. Whenever we feel hopeless, tired, weak, or confused, we can find all the refreshment we need in Christ Jesus. He is our hope and our strength, our eternal comfort, and perfect lover.

How can you find comfort in uncomfortable times?

Just Ask Him

I call to you, God, and you answer me.
Listen to me now, and hear what I say.
PSALM 17:6 NCV

Ah, the first crush. "Does he like me?" we wondered aloud to our friends. "Just ask him," they answered. "You may never know if you don't ask," they counseled. A note was written, folded, and passed. We waited nervously for the reply. The whole thing was simple, but also scary.

If only answers to prayer came so simply or quickly: "Should I take this job? Marry this man? Try to have a baby now, or in a year? Check yes or no." God's Word encourages us again and again to come to him with our questions, concerns, and deepest longings. He does promise a reply, though not necessarily in the form of a check in a box.

What are you longing to know? Just ask him. He's waiting expectantly for your prayers, and he will answer you. It may not be today, or even for a long time, but keep asking.

Pressing In

When hard pressed, I cried to the LORD;
he brought me into a spacious place.
The LORD is with me; I will not be afraid.
What can mere mortals do to me?

PSALM 118:5-6 NIV

Although the world's powers can appear indomitable, all the nations of the earth cannot stand against God. When we feel as if our backs are against the wall, or the pressures of the world are laying heavy upon us, we can call on God and he will answer us. He will deliver us out of our narrow confinement, the prison of our minds, or our earthly bonds, and release us into a spacious place where we can run free.

Even if God does not remove us from the trials we are facing, we can rest assured knowing that he uses everything for his glory and we will triumph in the end. The Lord is with us, and he answers when we call out to him. Nobody can steal the freedom and the joy that God gladly gives.

What are you afraid of?

Timely Words

A person finds joy in giving an apt reply—
and how good is a timely word!
PROVERBS 15:23 NIV

An appropriate word given at the right time is very beneficial both for the giver and the receiver. To obtain the sort of wisdom this requires does not come in a sudden burst of insight, but rather from quietly listening to God.

We do not suddenly become the answer during the situation. God has the answers, and we can only give them to others by learning from him. In meekness, we should hold back our own words and ask God what he would like to tell others through us.

Have you ever received a word that was so fitting at such an opportune moment that you knew it had to be wisdom from God that inspired it? How did that make you feel?

Firm Foundation

This is what the Sovereign LORD says:
"Look! I am placing a foundation stone in Jerusalem,
a firm and tested stone.
It is a precious cornerstone that is safe to build on.
Whoever believes need never be shaken."
ISAIAH 28:16 NLT

Architects know that for a building to stand it must first have a good foundation. This means digging down to the bedrock and supporting the weight by laying strong footings. Only then can a successful structure be built. Your Christian life is like that tower. God laid the foundation when you gave your life to him. Since that time, each bit of knowledge, every prayer, every verse has laid down the walls. When you obeyed him and showed his love to others the walls took shape. Slowly they rose, strong on the cornerstone of your faith and held together by God. Those walls keep the enemy away; they cannot be broken down or shaken.

You can take a brave stand in your relationships with others. Share what you know about the Lord and what he has done in your life. Don't be afraid of standing strong when the world mocks you. He is the firm foundation.

Do you feel God's strength when you are afraid? Do you remember a time when his power was working through you?

Repentance

The wages of sin is death,
but the free gift of God is eternal life
through Christ Jesus our Lord.
ROMANS 6:23 NLT

As humans, we sometimes wrongly judge sin on a scale. God does not view iniquity this way, however, since any imperfection separates us from a perfect God. We should refrain from comparing sin, judging others, or devaluing the grace that has been shown to us.

There is nobody who God's grace cannot extend to, if they would just be willing to receive it. As Christians, we should adamantly admit our need for God's grace and be willing to extend grace to others, regardless of how we weigh and measure their sin.

How did God's grace lead you to repentance?

Your Destiny

These things I plan won't happen right away. Slowly, steadily, surely, the time approaches when the vision will be fulfilled. If it seems slow, do not despair, for these things will surely come to pass. Just be patient! They will not be overdue a single day.

HABAKKUK 2:3 TLB

As we listen to a talented singer, or watch a brilliant athlete, these people, so apparently effortless in their pursuits, seem born for just those things. This is their destiny, we think. What is my destiny? we may then wonder. What was I born to do?

Whether or not you believe you have a specific purpose, God knows you do. And he knows just what it is, and how long—how many false starts and poor decisions—it will take you to fulfill it. He is deeply interested in the destinies of those who call him Father, just as he is in the ultimate fate of the whole world.

Are you waiting on God to fulfill—or reveal—your destiny?
Take comfort in the passage above, and thank him for his
perfect timing. If the waiting is hard, ask for his help.

Awesome Name

He provided redemption for his people;
he ordained his covenant forever—
holy and awesome is his name.

PSALM 111:9 NIV

As you wake to another morning, do you feel free from burdens or worn down by them? You might be experiencing some mountaintop moments and mornings are a joy, but if you are in a valley, mornings can be difficult.

Whatever your experience is right now, remember that God has redeemed you. He didn't just set the Israelites free, he set all of humanity free and made his promise of grace last forever. Let this covenant remind you of how awesome he is today so you are able to experience the light of this new life.

How can you share the good news of God's redemption
with those around you?

On the Calendar

Oh, that I had wings like a dove;
then I would fly away and rest!

PSALM 55:6 NLT

Back in our grandparents' era, life didn't seem as fast-paced as today. They actually used their front porches, visited with neighbors, family, and friends, and went on Sunday afternoon drives to enjoy the scenery. And that was despite not having all the labor-saving devices that we have today which actually don't seem to be helping a lot to give us restful lives.

Our calendars are crammed with commitments. We race from one place to another, annoyed that it took more than a minute at the fast food window or that the red light didn't change as quickly as anticipated. Halfway through the day, we're so tired we don't think we'll make it to the end of the day. We have to plan for rest just like we do everything else in our lives, because it won't just happen. Be intentional about setting time aside to spend with God. That's where real refreshment and strength come from, and those moments will make the remainder of your day so much better.

Do you feel guilty about taking a nap or resting?
Why or why not?

Give Me Joy

"Until now you have asked nothing in my name.
Ask, and you will receive, that your joy may be full."

JOHN 16:24 ESV

Birthday parties are so much fun. Imagine all the hoopla of games, party hats, songs, and cake. Oh, and the most exciting part: the presents! The highlight of every birthday party is when it is time to open the presents. The look of sheer joy on the birthday girl as she receives each gift is memorable. Who doesn't love getting gifts?

The definition of a gift is something given without the expectation of return. God wants to give you a wonderful gift—joy. The catch? He doesn't want you to strike a bargain. He doesn't want you to sacrifice anything. He just wants you to ask for it. It is so simple. When you don't feel you are worthy of joy, be brave and ask God for it anyway.

Are there things in your life you don't dare ask God for?
Can you take a step of faith and ask him for joy?

Slap Happy

*Go, eat your food with gladness, and drink your wine with a joyful heart,
for God has already approved what you do.*
ECCLESIASTES 9:7 NIV

Catherine was always a lot of fun. She lit up a room when she walked into it, and she had one of those personalities that made everyone around her feel good. She was sunshine to all who knew her. But there was a particular moment that all of her friends loved. They didn't come often, but when they did, they were something to behold. You see, when Catherine got really tired, she didn't become grouchy, she became slap happy. She would laugh until tears streamed down her face and she couldn't catch her breath. Everyone laughed with her. They couldn't help themselves. Her laughter was contagious.

The Bible says that a merry heart is like medicine to us. Maybe you can also help share that cheer and joy with others who need a hefty dose. Visit a shut-in or an elderly couple. Encourage someone who's going through a difficult time. Bring some sunshine into the life of a single mom. Those moments together will provide rest for their hearts and souls—and it will do the same for you.

*Why does laughter help you sleep better?
How can a joyful spirit be contagious to others?*

Successful Efforts

May the favor of the LORD our God rest on us;
establish the work of our hands for us—
yes, establish the work of our hands.
PSALM 90:17 NIV

Chances are that you will have to work in some shape or form today. You might be heading out to your job, volunteering for a community project, or just cleaning up around the home. Sometimes our list of jobs and chores seems endless and we wonder why we are stuck in this routine of maintenance!

Be encouraged to ask God the same thing this writer asks of him—to turn your work into something meaningful. Don't ever feel like your work isn't for a purpose. In some way, working is either benefiting you, or those you love. Try to approach your work with joy today.

How can God establish the work of your hands today?
How can he give you a good attitude and a resilient mind
and body to get through the day?

Love One Another

"A new commandment I give to you, that you love one another:
just as I have loved you, you also are to love one another."

JOHN 13:34 ESV

Christ came not only to free us from death, but also to save us from our destructive ways. He demonstrated for us the way to live and then asked that we follow his example. He taught us the perfect paradoxes between his kingdom and our selfish natures and invited us to live for others rather than ourselves. He loved us with an unrelenting love and told us to love others the same way.

To love one another is the trademark of the Christian life. We cannot claim to have known the love of Christ or to have heard his teachings if we fail to love each other because that is the basis of the Bible. God is love, and his followers will walk as he does.

Do you think the Scriptures would repeat the importance of loving people if it were easy? Who do you find difficult to love?

External Confidence

Let us then approach God's throne of grace with confidence,
so that we may receive mercy and find grace to help us in our time of need.
HEBREWS 4:16 NIV

Confidence can be defined in two ways. One is from within—we feel self-assured by our ability. The other is external—we believe we can rely on someone to do what they said they would. We cannot be brave without confidence, but the confidence we need does not come from the first definition. It is not wise to conjure up feelings of bravery through self-assurance of our own abilities, for they inevitability will fail us.

To succeed in life, our confidence must come from a firm trust in Jesus Christ, what he did for us on the cross, and how he continues to intercede for us. Our confidence does not come from our own power, but from Christ-given power. Walk into every situation today knowing that you have immediate, VIP access to throne of God, and there is an abundant warehouse of grace and mercy waiting for you.

What self-assurance do you need to trade
for God's assurance today?

Choosing Compassion

You, LORD, are a compassionate and gracious God,
slow to anger, abounding in love and faithfulness.
PSALM 86:15 NIV

Consider the Israelites wandering in the desert: God had rescued them out of bondage and goes before them in a pillar of fire, providing for their every need and protecting them. What do they offer to him? Complaints. Listen to the psalms of David—the man after God's own heart—as he lays his burdens at the feet of God, praising his majesty and might. But what does David do when he wants what he cannot have? Steals, murders, and lies. Paul, who gave his life to preach the gospel he loved to people near and far, shares the astounding gift of God's grace to Jews and Gentiles alike. But who was he before his conversion? A hateful, persecuting murderer of Christians.

God loves his children regardless of their sin, their past, and their failings. We aren't dealt with as we deserve; rather, according to his great love for us. Can we say the same about how we treat those around us?

Are you compassionate, slow to anger, and full of love?
Or are you offended, impatient, and aggravated?

Any Circumstance

Not that I speak from want,
for I have learned to be content in whatever circumstances I am.
PHILIPPIANS 4:11 NASB

Contentment is not a natural response to being without; it is a mindset that is learned from relying on God. When we undergo seasons of being in need, we learn more intimately how fulfilling God is and how faith in him is really what carries us through the most challenging times.

Rather than turning to worldly answers first, we should learn contentment and trust. When circumstances cannot steal our contentment because of our confidence in God's care, it fills us with true joy and peace.

How can you practice contentment today?

Being Brave

"Have I not commanded you? Be strong and courageous.
Do not be afraid; do not be discouraged, for the LORD your God
will be with you wherever you go."

JOSHUA 1:9 NIV

Courage! As a Christian you can be strong, secure in who you are
as God's child. You show compassion to those in need, love to those
around you, and think pure thoughts. You are kind and generous;
you speak truth and don't compare yourself to other people.
When the enemy sends his darts your way, you stand firm, you are
persistently seeking your heavenly Father's help. You read the Word
regularly and remember God's promises and obey him. You look
forward to heaven and are grateful for your salvation.

Worry and anxiety flee as you give over your troubles to the Lord.
You have the courage to be bold in proclaiming your faith. Blessed
are you that in time of fear and discouragement you have the Lord to
help and guide you through all your days. You are a child of the King
of the universe!

*Do you see yourself in these descriptions? Which are you
confident about? Are there areas you need to work on?*

Ark of Strength

Arise, O LORD, to Your resting place,
You and the ark of Your strength.
PSALM 132:8 NASB

*D*avid was a keen worshipper, but he also had a great reason to dance! The ark of the covenant was back in his possession and having the Lord's presence with him meant that God's favor was with David and his kingdom. He had a huge reason to celebrate.

You have a reason to celebrate too. The presence of God is with you—he is in your heart—and that means his favor is with you. Dance before the Lord like no one is watching today! Thank God for sending his Son, Jesus, who made a way for his presence to live inside of you.

How does the joy of knowing that you have God's strength, power, and grace within you give you an extra spring in your step?

This Is the Day

This is the day the LORD has made.
We will rejoice and be glad in it.
PSALM 118:24 NLT

When winter is fully upon us, it is not as warm outside, and there's not as much life in nature. If you live where winter is cold, you may be growing tired of boots, hats, scarves (well, maybe not scarves), and puffy, shapeless coats. Looking outside, there may not be much to feel particularly joyful about.

The simple truth is that God made today, and he made it with you in it. As you go into your day today, either with excitement or dread, encourage yourself that this is a day purposed by the Lord, for you. Make the most out of it!

Even if you weren't that happy to get out of bed, how can you commit your day to God and thank him for making it?

Aching Bones

Have mercy on me, LORD, for I am faint;
heal me, LORD, for my bones are in agony.
PSALM 6:2 NIV

Did you have trouble getting up this morning? Maybe it was too dark, you had a late night, or your bones were too achy to want to move! Our lifestyle doesn't allow us to just stay in bed as long as we need to, there are kids, jobs, or classes to attend to and those things don't wait for you.

We are prone to staying up too late, forgetting to eat breakfast, and generally just rushing around a lot. This can make us faint and tired by the end of the day. Ask the Lord for energy, and then make some wise choices about your schedule so you can endure the day ahead.

When you are feeling tired and sore, how do you seek wisdom to do the healthiest things for your body and mind?

Embracing Weakness

Humble yourselves in the sight of the Lord,
and He will lift you up.
JAMES 4:10 NKJV

*D*o you ever find yourself suddenly aware of your own glaring weaknesses? Aware that, if left up to your own good works, you wouldn't stand a chance of attaining salvation? We should find great comfort in the fact that we are nothing without salvation in Christ Jesus.

Thankfully, God made a way for us to be united with him, despite impatience, selfishness, anger, and pride. God deeply cares for us and patiently sustains us with steady, faithful, and adoring love. Amazingly, his love even goes beyond this to embrace and transform our weakness when we yield it to him. Weakness isn't something to be feared or hidden; weakness submitted to God allows the power of Christ to work in and through us. When we know our weakness, we are more aware of our need for his strength. When we put ourselves in a position of humility and ask him to be strong where we are weak, he is delighted to help.

*How can you submit your weakness to God so that,
through him, you can be strong?*

Be Sure

Know that the LORD has set apart
his faithful servant for himself;
the LORD hears when I call to him.

PSALM 4:3 NIV

Do you know those people that seem to be confident about everything they say and do? Do you sometimes wish to be as confident as they are? Being confident isn't the same as being prideful or arrogant. It is an inner peace and acceptance of who you are, and it is something that can't be shaken by external opinions or judgements.

This verse exudes confidence, "The Lord hears when I call to him." This confidence can only come from someone who is so sure of how much they are accepted and loved that they know their God will hear them. May this be your confidence today and always.

How can you know that God hears you when you call to him?

Unfailing Goodness

"I am about to go the way of all the earth, and you know in your hearts and souls, all of you, that not one thing has failed of all the good things that the LORD your God promised concerning you; all have come to pass for you, not one of them has failed."

JOSHUA 23:14 NRSV

Do you remember the first thing that you failed at? Maybe it was a test at school, a diet, a job interview, or even a relationship. Failure is difficult to admit, especially in a culture that values outward success and appearance. We often hear it said that success comes from many failures, but we only really hear that from successful people!

When Joshua was "advanced in years," he reminded the Israelites of all that God had done for them. Though they had been unfaithful to God many times, God remained faithful, and they became a great nation that none could withstand. God had a plan and a purpose for the nation of Israel, and through his power and mercy he ensured that these plans succeeded. In the same way, God has a purpose for your life, and while you may fail, he will not.

How can you take the opportunity today to
submit your heart to God's will?

Crazy

In peace I will lie down and sleep,
for you alone, LORD,
make me dwell in safety.

PSALM 4:8 NIV

Do you sometimes have moments when you accomplish a tremendous amount, and for just a few minutes you feel like Wonder Woman? Unfortunately, those are often rare moments—mainly because we pack our schedules so full of things that it's ridiculous. We can do it all and do it all well. Right? It doesn't matter if we've been up sick all night. It doesn't matter if a family emergency is thrown into the mix, or if a snowstorm or hurricane blows through town. We will get it all done or we'll die trying. Are we crazy?

Why do we put such unrealistic expectations on ourselves? What even possessed us to think we could do the work of sixteen people? In a single day. With perfect results. And with our lipstick still on. It's time for a come-to-Jesus moment. Literally. Bring your calendars, schedules, and lists, and give them all to him. Ask him to be the keeper of your schedule, to show you what he wants you to do—and not do.

Do you have trouble saying no when someone asks you to do something? Can you start praying before answering?

Promised Grace

I have sought Your favor with all my heart;
be gracious to me according to your promise.
PSALM 119:58 NIV

Do you wake up in the morning full of worries over decisions you need to make? Sometimes our hearts can be in turmoil because we lack knowing the right thing to do.

When God seems absent in the answers, choose to see it as an invitation to seek him more. Seek his favor with all your heart. As this Scripture says, he has promised to be gracious, so be encouraged to continue to look for his help. Seek his favor today even if you don't know exactly what he wants you to say or do.

How can you choose to trust in God's promises and grace, knowing that even if you are unsure, God is not?

Thrive in Winter

To everything there is a season,
A time for every purpose under heaven.
ECCLESIASTES 3:1 NKJV

Winter can be a time of inactivity. For farmers, winter is their slow season. For others, just the snow, rain, and chill make it difficult to be outside. But stillness and slowness do not mean nothing is happening. In nature, things are always happening below the surface. Birds are still eating, animals are still sleeping, and trout are still swimming under frozen ice.

Sometimes slowing down can be one of the most powerful acts in the life of a believer. It is a declaration of trust that the one who made us is still working and fighting for us. We allow the work and the seeds he has planted in us to grow and take even greater root in our hearts. Sometimes in our stillness, we have the greatest victories over our giants because we exhibit trust that God is still moving mightily.

Can you believe God is working, even in winter,
or have you become a complainer?

Stillness

Let all that I am wait quietly before God,
for my hope is in him.

PSALM 62:5 NLT

*D*usk settles on a chilly winter night. A gray fog hovers and snow begins to fall: cold, blustering snow…the kind that sticks. The snow keeps coming until you can barely see one hundred feet in front of you. In the woods it's quiet; all you can hear is the gentle wind, and all you can see is snow and trees. A pure white blanket of snow restores the earth, and as it falls, it restores you.

Sometimes we have to get outside of the noise and chaos of our own four walls. We have to step out into the snow, or the sun, or the breeze. We have to get alone, get silent, and clear the clutter from our minds and hearts as we stand in God's natural sanctuary. There is so much power in the stillness of knowing God as you stand serene in the world he created. The busyness of your life will always be there, but never forget to take the moments you can, to stop and know your God.

*Do you find that the moments you spend with God
help you find refreshment and strength to take on
whatever will come next?*

Our Gatekeeper

Don't copy the behavior and customs of this world, but let God transform you into a new person by changing the way you think. Then you will learn to know God's will for you, which is good and pleasing and perfect.

ROMANS 12:2 NLT

*E*very day we are surrounded by so much noise from the outside world. Messages are loud and relentless—how we should look, act, and think. Culture has its own set of rules and ideals, many of which differ from God's. Influences come at us in so many forms. Social pressure, media, politics, even close friendships. We process a high volume of information every day. Ideals can impact our characters and decisions. They can shape who we are and what we believe in. They can drown out God's voice.

It is so important to center ourselves in Christ and surround ourselves with positive influences. Our hearts need to be immersed in his Word, so he can transform our minds with truth. And we can learn how to decipher what is from him and what is not.

Who is influencing your thoughts today? Is your mind protected from the influence of the outside world by being immersed in God's Word?

February

The name of the Lord is a strong fortress;
the godly run to him and are safe.

Proverbs 18:10 nlt

Choose Joy

A cheerful heart puts a smile on your face,
but a broken heart leads to depression.
PROVERBS 15:13 TPT

*E*veryone experiences deep sadness and disappointment in life. Sometimes it may seem your life is full of them. You can't catch a break. Take heart when you experience trials and nothing goes your way. Broken promises, relationships, and disappointments can seem an unending theme. Our Father has promised us joy. He understands joy and sadness more than we know. God's Word says that when we are sad, our spirit is broken. Don't let it stop there. Find joy! Look for joy! Choose joy!

In the Bible, joy is mentioned over 250 times. When you feel broken, you can choose joy—the joy of the Lord—and it will be the strength you need. When all happiness is taken from you, choose the joy of the Lord! When you are hurting, look to the joy of the Lord and bravely move in another direction. Make a new friend. Help a neighbor. Pay for a stranger's coffee order. Choose joy—the strength you need to repair a broken spirit.

Can you see how helping others might bring you joy?
Can you see past your own circumstances to be a blessing
to someone with a broken spirit?

Love Bubbling Over

May the Lord make your love increase and overflow
for each other and for everyone else,
just as ours does for you.
1 THESSALONIANS 3:12 NIV

Five-year-old Emma eyed the big tub in her mama's bathroom. Mama had said Emma needed a bath. She hadn't mentioned a bubble bath, but Emma didn't think she'd mind. She turned the faucet on and dumped a whole bottle of bubble bath under the stream of water: the gallon-sized economy bottle. Her eyes got big as she saw the tub filling with bubbles. This was going to be awesome. Her mama hadn't ever had this many bubbles before. Emma ran to get what she needed for her bath, but she was soon distracted.

When she skipped back down the hall to put to her parents' room, her little jaw dropped in shock. Bubbles were floating out of the bathroom. Into the bedroom and across the floor. Emma's overflow of bathwater and bubbles definitely wasn't planned. But you know what? God wants us to have an overflow in our lives. He wants us to live so close to him that his sweetness wears off on us. And then he wants our love to increase and overflow into the lives of others.

Why are you sometimes hesitant to tell others about Jesus?
Does it make you anxious?

I Told you

"From the beginning I told you what would happen in the end.
A long time ago I told you things that have not yet happened.
When I plan something, it happens. What I want to do, I will do."

ISAIAH 46:10 NCV

God does not back down from what he says will happen. He does not exaggerate, he does not keep the secret from those he ordains to know. We know he is all-powerful, and we know he is just to declare his will and fulfill it. It is our duty and response to worship him and do his will.

The words of God are gracious to embolden us to response. We know Jesus loves us, and we know he is firm in his resolve to be Lord. It is not that we get a vote; he is Lord, and he will always remain in charge. We do have free will, though. It is our joy and privilege to offer and maintain that he is Lord of what we choose in our hearts to do. Let our responses be in line with what God chooses, says, and does. Jesus is our example in this.

What do you need to do to understand or fulfill God's will for you? What is your action step right now?

Congregation

Praise the LORD!
I will give thanks to the LORD with my whole heart,
in the company of the upright, in the congregation.

PSALM 111:1 ESV

*G*od had a purpose to fulfil through the people of Israel. He intended this community of people to be part of revealing his plan for humanity. They needed to reconnect with one another so they could be unified in their covenant with the one true God.

There is a certain specialness to reuniting with our family and friends on those occasions we can all be together in one place. When we are together with people who share the same values, stories, and even similar humor, it makes life feel more meaningful. Think about the community that you feel closest to and make an effort to get in touch today. God doesn't want us to do life alone. There is strength and unity in the gathering of people who love one another.

How can you connect with others so you can enjoy and encourage each other today?

A Steady Heart

*They will not live in fear or dread of what may come,
for their hearts are firm, ever secure in their faith.*
PSALM 112:7 TPT

God has asked you a specific thing. As you begin to put the legwork behind the calling he has given you, you cannot expect the road to be without opposition. Maybe God has asked you to take a step and adopt a child, start a business, plant a church, put your kids in public school, move, or lead a small group. The possibilities are endless, but the end is the same—all for the glory of God. In moving toward what God wants you to do, the forces of darkness will move back.

Can you steady your heart when people whisper behind your back or criticize your actions? Can you steady your heart when you fail along the way? Can you steady your heart when others fail you? Our hearts can be firm as a rock when we trust that God is working and moving on our behalf. If he has placed something on your heart today, don't let fear of what could happen get in your way. Step out in faith and anchor your heart in the Lord.

*What "what-if" scenarios do you need to silence
and bring before God today?*

Shadowed

Because you are my helper,
I sing for joy in the shadow of your wings.
PSALM 63:7 NLT

*G*od is our greatest cheerleader. He watches as we take flight in a calling he has put before us, and he gently encourages us, urging us forward and cheering us on.

The God of the universe, the Creator of everything, the one living on the throne of righteousness, knows us and cheers us on. What a privilege and an honor to know that once he sets us down a path, he will not let us stray without first urging us forward for his mission. You can walk safely in the shadow of his wings every day because he is your shield and protector.

How does God help you in times of trouble and times of joy?

In your Hand

Let them praise the LORD,
because they were created by his command.
PSALM 148:5 NCV

God wants to use you in so many different ways, be it in your daily life or in a specific mission that he sets out for you. God doesn't, however, want you to try and be like somebody else in the way that you approach things. You don't have to talk like a famous preacher or lead a Bible study like your friend. You don't have to sing in the band to be influential.

God needs you to be you! He wants you to wear the things that make you who you are in order to do his work. David couldn't wear Saul's armor; he just needed his everyday attire to get the job done. Wear your own shoes as you walk into today's tasks and be proud of them. God has given you a specific personality, set of experiences, style, and opportunities that are uniquely yours.

How can you be comfortable with the person you have become and use your unique self to accomplish God's will?

World Masters

You made them rulers over the works of your hands;
you put everything under their feet.
PSALM 8:6 NIV

*G*od's creation is beautiful and astounding, but he put extra special effort into making humanity. Not only are we created with beauty and intricacy, but we also have been given the status of being special because we are the ones that have been made in God's image.

Every part of nature reveals something of God, and we are the pinnacle of this revelation displayed perfectly through Jesus. If you are feeling insignificant or weak this morning, remind yourself that God has chosen to show himself through you. Now that is a significant job!

How can you thank God for choosing to reveal himself through you? How can you be bold in your faith today, knowing that God has created you with an important purpose in mind?

Ruled with Grace

The law was brought in so that the trespass might increase.
But where sin increased, grace increased all the more,
so that, just as sin reigned in death, so also grace might reign through
righteousness to bring eternal life through Jesus Christ our Lord.
ROMANS 5:20-21 NIV

*G*od's law was given so that people could see how sinful they were. But instead, we began to sin more and more. You'd think God would've given up on us, but instead, he gave us grace in abundance. We make terrible decision after terrible decision, and still he loves us and shows his mercy.

Though we deserve to be punished for our faults, God rules with his wonderful grace. Jesus died so that we would be given the gift of eternal life in heaven. Think of all the sacrifices you make for others, and then consider what it would take to sacrifice yourself so that others could live. Talk about the gift of a lifetime!

Spend some time thanking the Lord for the great gift he has given you today. What sacrifices has he made for you?

Lost and Found

"So will you also pass through a time of intense sorrow when I am taken from you, but you will see me again! And then your hearts will burst with joy, with no one being able to take it from you!"

JOHN 16:22 TPT

Grief is something that no one wants to experience, but while we live in a broken world, it will come to us. Perhaps you have experienced a broken relationship, loss of a loved one, or a move from one city to another. There are many experiences of loss and they are all followed by grief. We don't need to fear the experience of grief; it is a natural and common human experience and we are never alone in feeling this way.

Jesus acknowledged that we will experience grief, but it comes with a reassurance that there will be a day when our joy will be complete, and we will no longer experience loss. So be brave, child of God, that while you experience heartbreak on earth, Jesus will restore your joy to you. Cling to him in your anguish and rejoice in your blessings. He is with you in it all.

How have you experienced Jesus in the middle of your despair?

Blizzard of Responsibility

There is a special rest still waiting for the people of God.
For all who have entered into God's rest have rested from their labors,
just as God did after creating the world.

HEBREWS 4:9-10 NLT

Have you ever experienced a blizzard? Snow comes down so fast that you can't see through the thick blanket of white flakes. The wind howls about, blowing snow in every direction. As the intensity of the storm continues, fluffy whiteness begins to pile up, first in inches and then in feet, until everyone is stuck where they are as the blizzard seemingly rages out of control.

Have you ever thought about the fact that our lives are similar to those blizzards? Responsibilities come into our days much like those snowflakes. Some days it's like the beginning of a snowstorm with a gentle stream of tasks. On other days, it's like a blizzard of responsibilities that pile up. Just as God is in control of the blizzards, he's in control of our lives. He cares when we feel overwhelmed. He's given us a sweet promise of rest. Spending time in his Word and turning on some calming worship music can take us from feeling stuck in a blizzard of craziness to a blizzard of sweet joy.

Why is balance important for you? How does taking on too many responsibilities affect you and those around you?

Rest in Jesus

Protect me from harm;
keep an eye on me like you would a child
reflected in the twinkling of your eye.
Yes, hide me within the shelter of your embrace,
under your outstretched wings.

PSALM 17:8 TPT

Have you ever been awake when you think no one else is? Maybe you had an early morning flight, and you feel you are the only person who could possibly be stirring at that hour. It feels kind of magical, doesn't it? It's like you have an unshared secret. Regardless of you being a night owl, morning person, or somewhere in-between, there is peace that comes with meeting Jesus in secret— when your world has stopped for a bit.

Whatever it looks like, rising early or staying up late, taking a work break, a study break, or a mommy break, finding that quiet is where you can actually acquire strength. We need spiritual food to conquer each day.

Can you find daily quiet time to meet with Jesus? He will meet you in that space, filling you with peace, strength, and love to go out and conquer the world.

Laugh Out Loud

When the cares of my heart are many,
your consolations cheer my soul.
PSALM 94:19 ESV

Have you ever been in the middle of a stressful time and then something made you laugh until your stomach hurt? Isn't it amazing how the cares of life float away when that happens? It's especially awesome to hear someone whose laughter is so contagious that everyone is soon laughing with them. When was the last time you had an all-out belly laugh? Most of us don't have enough of those. Do you snort when you laugh or is your laughter dainty and giggle-like? Types of laughter vary so much that there are more than a dozen words to describe different forms of laughter. No matter how you laugh, it's always good for whatever ails you.

While laughter won't alleviate the causes of stress in your life, it can help you feel better, which in turn leads to relaxation and the renewed ability to face what's going on. Mental health professionals have researched and compiled quite a list of the healthy benefits of laughter. God made laughter and he wants us to enjoy it.

How has God used laughter to help you get through stressful times? Why do you think God tied laughter and improved health together?

I Love you

I love you, LORD, my strength.

PSALM 18:1

*I*t is three simple words, yet they can hold such power, beauty, and hope. God is love and we will never stop learning about what this means to us. Today, however, think of your love for God and what he means to you. There are so many reasons why we love God, but perhaps you could just simply express those three words to him and let your adoration for him be enough.

On this day when you are reminded of people's love for each other, don't forget to acknowledge the one who is defined in his very nature as love, and offer this love unconditionally to you. Dwell in his love.

How do you show the Lord that you love him?

Sweet Like Taffy

When my spirit faints within me,
you know my way!
PSALM 142:3 ESV

There's a candy place that has large windows around its store. Folks watch with interest as caramel apples are dipped and fudge is made. There are also days when they make taffy. A sugar syrup is cooked and then flavors and colors are added. The candy-maker flips and folds it with a spatula until it's cool enough to handle. The candy is rolled into a rope-like shape and then pulled and twisted—again and again and again until the taffy becomes glossy. After several more steps, it's rolled into a rope shape, cut into pieces, and wrapped in paper.

You might not realize it, but we are like taffy. Have you had days where it's felt as if you've been pulled in a dozen different directions? It's stressful, especially when we were already exhausted before all the pulling began. Our spirits are faint within us, and we need to get rid of the stress. When we're in the midst of these times, God says he knows our way. He can strengthen us, refresh us, and give us joy as we're pulled from task to task.

How does stress affect you when you feel like you're being pulled in a dozen different directions?

Rest for the Exhausted

Those who hope in the LORD will renew their strength.
They will soar on wings like eagles;
they will run and not grow weary,
they will walk and not be faint.

ISAIAH 40:31 NIV

Have you ever been totally exhausted and all you wanted was to go to bed and rest? For some, overwhelming tiredness is from long days at work with overtime thrown in. After months of an unrelenting schedule, we can become so weary that when we go to bed at night, we can't get to sleep for hours because our minds kept whirling with all the details of the day. When we finally fall asleep, it feels like we only sleep for minutes before it's time to get up again.

The good news is that God promises to give us rest and renew our strength. But we also have to learn to say no when faced with decisions. We don't have to work all the overtime. Balance is necessary. That's where it's helpful to pray about our choices before we say yes to adding new tasks to our already busy days. If we allow God to make those decisions for us, he promises us something beyond amazing: rest for the weary.

Why is it so hard to say no when opportunities come your way?

Guard It

Take control of what I say, O LORD,
and guard my lips.
PSALM 141:3 NIV

Have you ever found yourself drawn in to a negative conversation about someone else? You might not have started the conversation but as it goes on you realize that you are contributing more than is wise to. Be encouraged to address those moments and not let them slip by. It's important that we don't compromise our integrity, not because we should feel obligated to do the right thing, but because we want the love of Christ to always be front and center of our conversations and attitudes.

Your mouth can bring harm but it can also bring an incredible amount of good, so be encouraged to bless others through your words.

How can you let God's love come before anything you say?

Awake at Night

I lie awake,
I have become like a lonely bird on a housetop.
PSALM 102:7 NASB

Have you had one of those nights when you just didn't feel like you slept at all? Perhaps you kept checking the clock and seeing that only an hour had passed since the last time you checked. These nights can be laden with anxiety. No one else is awake and you are alone with your thoughts and feelings.

If you could picture that bird alone on a housetop, it would look a lot like you are feeling in those moments: solitary, waiting, watching. In those times of feeling alone, remember that your God is a God who never sleeps. He cares so much for you that he is ready to listen to your heart at any time. Use it as an opportunity to engage your Creator and get some insight and wisdom from him.

Do you know that the Father cares for you even more than the lonely bird on the rooftop? How can you listen to him in your moments of loneliness?

Living Word

The word of God is living and active and sharper than any two-edged
sword, and piercing as far as the division of soul and spirit, of both joints
and marrow, and able to judge the thoughts and intentions of the heart.

HEBREWS 4:12 NASB

*D*oes God sometimes speak to you in themes? We all go through
different seasons in life, and God speaks to our hearts accordingly.
Some of us may be going through a season of learning to wait, while
another is learning how to step out in faith. But the beautiful thing
about God is that he is big enough to speak to all of us—in our
different places, with our different hearts—at the same time, with
the same words.

God's Word is alive and active. It can deliver truth to the heart of
each unique person. Two people can get something completely
different from the same passage of Scripture because of what God
has been doing in each of their hearts separately. Through the body
of Christ, we can come together and share what God is teaching
us—multiplying our individual growth as we encourage one another.

*How can you ensure that you never doubt the power of what
you hold in your hands when you read the Word of God?*

Mixed Messages

With the tongue we praise our Lord and Father, and with it we curse
human beings, who have been made in God's likeness. Out of the same
mouth come praise and cursing. My brothers and sisters, this should not
be. Can both fresh water and salt water flow from the same spring? My
brothers and sisters, can a fig tree bear olives, or a grapevine bear figs?
Neither can a salt spring produce fresh water.

JAMES 3:9-12 NIV

Have you ever spent Sunday morning in a pew, proclaiming your
love for God, then walked out and said to a friend, "Did you see
Sally's skirt? It was so short!" Perhaps you judged as someone darted
in fifteen minutes late to the service. Maybe you told yourself that
you're a better person than Susie because Susie yells at her kids and
you rarely yell at anybody.

If so, you're not alone. It's our natural tendency to put others
down to make ourselves feel better. We hold the secret belief that
if someone else looks bad, we'll look good by comparison. But the
Bible tells us that we cannot praise Jesus and curse others at the
same time.

*How can you keep careful watch over your thoughts and words
today, being sure to lift others up as you climb closer to God?*

Don't Be Ashamed

I am suffering now because I tell the Good News, but I am not ashamed, because I know Jesus, the One in whom I have believed. And I am sure he is able to protect what he has trusted me with until that day.

2 TIMOTHY 1:12 NCV

Have you ever tried to wade upstream through a river, or swim against a strong current? It is hard! Sometimes this is how we can feel as a Christian in a world full of unbelievers. Our modern culture is full of political correctness and accepting all beliefs, but when it comes to Christianity, it can feel like anything we say is offensive!

Paul was put in prison a number of times for offending the people of his time. He seemed to suffer gladly because he was convinced that Jesus was the Savior and that his mission was to share this good news with the world. Paul was convinced of the truth, and because of this, he was not ashamed!

Do you tend to keep quiet about your faith in Jesus? Are you worried about suffering, or being mocked for your beliefs? Take time each day to develop your relationship with him; the more you know Jesus, the more confident you will be in what you believe.

Cheer for the Prize

May the God who gives endurance and encouragement give you the same attitude of mind toward each other that Christ Jesus had.

ROMANS 15:5 NIV

Have you ever watched cheerleaders at a sporting event? Smiling, bubbly, energetic, yelling for their beloved team. What we don't see is what might be going on underneath all of that encouragement. Everyone has their issues. And yet there they are, faithfully devoted to their team because they know the prize at the end.

In this same way, let us encourage one another in our faith. Imagine our Abba Father's joy when he sees us lifting each other up in praise and loving despite whatever we might have going on. There is so much to be gained in relationship with other believers whether on the receiving or giving end. And the prize at the end is eternity. There is nothing greater.

What are some ways you can encourage others?
Think of the delight in God's heart when he sees you
giving your time and talents.

Wailing to Whirling

*You have turned my mourning into joyful dancing.
You have taken away my clothes of mourning
and clothed me with joy.*
PSALM 30:11 NLT

Have you experienced driving through a really long tunnel and only knowing that there was an end because of the number markings on the wall or your GPS telling you it was coming to an end? If you didn't have any idea, those tunnels could seem really long and a little bit scary.

Grief and heartache can sometimes feel like an endless tunnel with little to tell you how long or how much more you will have to endure. If this is you right now, find courage in the psalm above— of one who has found the joy and light at the end of their tunnel. It does happen, and it will happen for you. Your mourning will one day turn to joy.

How can you choose to be strengthened by the hope that your mourning can be turned to joy? How do you keep trusting God while you are in the middle of it?

Extinguish the Fire

A gentle answer will calm a person's anger,
but an unkind answer will cause more anger.
PROVERBS 15:1 NCV

Have you mastered the art of making a fire? Even if you haven't done it yourself, you will know that fire needs kindling and a bit of oxygen before it starts to really take off. As you feed the fire, you cause it to grow and become stronger. This is how the Scriptures liken our response to anger.

If we response with anger or defensiveness and show no grace, it will add just the right elements to make that person even more upset. Think of the last time you had an argument and how hard it was to control things from getting worse. If we can take a moment to pause, keep calm, and respond with grace and gentleness, we will help to calm the other person. It's worth trying.

Can you think of ways to respond the next time you are confronted with someone's anger? Having a strategy before the scenario happens can help prepare you for a good response.

Known Before

> "Before I formed you in the womb I knew you."
> JEREMIAH 1:4 NIV

His mother told him he was a mistake: a baby no one had intended, a gender discouraged, a timing unlikely. What was he to think? One day, he saw this verse. He knew God had planned him from the beginning of the ages. He was perfect in God's sight, respected and loved, and set apart for greatness. Had he not been— had he not become the exquisite person he is today—the world would be sadly different.

You are this man, in many, many ways. Upon your words, your actions, and your being, springs a world of possibilities only God is genius enough to imagine and ordain. You are very, very precious. Do not ever despise yourself in any way. You are good enough for God, and that is enough by far.

How can you celebrate who you are today?
Be brave if you must!

Relationships

Spend time with the wise and you will become wise,
but the friends of fools will suffer.
PROVERBS 13:20 NCV

Humans were created for relationship; we are hardwired to want and need others. Because of our design, friendships are vitally important to our lives and also to our walk with God. It is a widely known fact that friends either bring us up or drag us down. Likewise, friends can either encourage or discourage us in our pursuit of godliness.

As we seek counsel from our friends for the decisions we make in life, it is important that those friends are pushing us to follow Christ and not our own desires. Your friends have the power to lead you closer to God or push you away from him. Surround yourself with people who will echo God's words to you rather than lead you off course with their advice.

Evaluate yourself to make sure you are being the kind of friend who will lead others closer to Christ by your influence and your advice.

Devoted Disciple

They were continually devoting themselves to the apostles' teaching and to fellowship, to the breaking of bread and to prayer.

ACTS 2:42 NASB

If there's one verse to make a church group feel guilty, it's this one. It's hard to imagine how any of us could live like this in our day and age. Imagine a constant stream of teaching, eating, and praying with your Christian friends. To some that might sound pleasant, but for many, it sounds impossible. Read between the lines. Of course, these people had homes, families, and the routines of life, just like we do.

The idea of continual devotion is simply the positive routines and habits that the believers dedicated themselves to—much like the habits we try to form in our Christian faith. We read devotionals, we pray, we go to church, we serve or gather with church groups. If this isn't part of your life, be encouraged to make a habit of it. Believers need each other, and they are encouraged by the devotion of others.

How can you become more engaged with believers this week?

By your Walk

How priceless is your unfailing love, O God!
People take refuge in the shadow of your wings.
They feast on the abundance of your house;
you give them drink from your river of delights.

PSALM 36:7-8 NIV

If you are fortunate enough to live near an ocean, you've seen people walking up and down the jagged line of wave meeting sand. Some walk alone but often in pairs. Imagine sitting on the shore, when you spy a couple walking a pole's length apart, casting dirty glances at each other. Or maybe one is stomping ahead and the other is trying to catch up. Deep down those two might be in love, but you sure wouldn't guess it by their walk, would you? Then you see another couple, her hand gently wrapped around his forearm, their pace in perfect tune. We judge relationships by the way people walk.

What does your walk with Christ say about your relationship with him? Does it speak of years of perseverance, of walking the path of life with him and being filled with joy in his presence? Or are you stomping your feet and scowling every step of the way, with more duty than love? Stop today and ask yourself, where is the joy?

Is your Christian walk filled with joy?

March

He gives strength to the weary
and increases the power of the weak.

ISAIAH 40:29 NIV

Hunger for God

Like newborn babies, crave pure spiritual milk,
so that by it you may grow up in your salvation.
2 PETER 3:18 NIV

If you have ever taken a minute to observe a hungry infant, you have seen just how desperate they can be. It doesn't matter if a bottle is delayed by one minute or ten, the reaction of hunger holds the same intensity. The need to eat is relentless and demanding. The cry for food is most often loud, angry, and repetitive. The craving so strong that their natural instinct is to fight for it.

As soon as they taste milk on their lips, though, they quiet and relax. Soon after their need to eat is satisfied, they surrender to a peaceful sleep. They are content, because in that moment they were fed. Milk is essential to every part of a baby's healthy development. Our need for the Lord's Word is akin to that of an infant's need for milk. We are dependent on it for survival, and yet we have come accustomed to pacifying that need with other distractions. How strong would our faith be if we took the spiritual food that our souls crave? God wants us to be strong, to be healthy, and to be fed.

Do you crave God's Word?
Or are you pacifying the need in other ways?

Small Stuff

*What are mere mortals that you should think about them,
human beings that you should care for them?*
PSALM 8:4 NLT

If you have ever watched a scientific program about our universe, you will likely feel overwhelmed by how colossal and complex our universe and surrounding galaxies are! It can make humans seem tiny and insignificant when you consider that as a planet, earth is nothing in comparison to the vastness of the rest of the cosmos!

What are mere mortals that God would think about us; why would he care? Genesis tells us that God made us in his image—that has to be pretty special. He created us with intention; he created us to be like him and to live in relationship with him. He created us for love. Let his love for you overwhelm you today.

*How significant do you feel in light of this universe?
Do you know that God's Word says that he adores you?*

Steady Steps

The LORD makes firm the steps
of the one who delights in him.
PSALM 37:23 NIV

If you've ever taken the hand of a toddler, you'll know that they are relying on you for their balance. If they stumble, you can easily steady them. This simple act of holding a hand means that you and the child have confidence that they won't fall flat on their face.

In the same way, when we commit our way to the Lord, we are essentially placing our hand in his. He delights in the fact that we are walking with him and even in the times when we stumble, he will steady our path and give us the confidence to keep walking.

Do you find it difficult to invite Jesus to take your hand and stand beside you each day? Do you understand what it means for him to keep your steps firm and keep you from falling?

Mercy and Grace

God still loved us with such great love. He is so rich in compassion and
mercy Even when we were dead and doomed in our many sins, he united
us into the very life of Christ and saved us by his wonderful grace!

EPHESIANS 2:4-5 TPT

Imagine a courtroom; directly in front of you sits a stern judge in
a black robe. You stand, knees knocking and anxious. You can hardly
breathe. You know you are guilty. There is a roaring in your ears.
It is just a matter of how much time you will serve in prison. Your
life as you know it is effectively over. BANG! The gavel comes down
and the judge says, "Pardoned." Oh, the joy that fills your heart. The
heartfelt elation enters your whole being. It is hard to take in.

When we realize that even in the middle of our sins God showered
us with unfathomable mercy and grace by sending Jesus to die in
our place, it should be apparent to us that we should extend both
grace and mercy to those who offend us. The grievance may be
small or immense. It may even seem insurmountable. By offering
forgiveness we help ourselves more than the offender. It isn't easy,
but when we look to God's example of love, we can trust that it is to
our benefit to model him.

*How has God's model of mercy and grace made a difference in
your life? Do you find it easy to forgive others?*

What He Says

Mary responded, "I am the Lord's servant.
May everything you have said about me come true."
And then the angel left her.

LUKE 1:38 NLT

*I*n a memorable scene from a movie about teenage girls, a teacher asks a gymnasium full of young women to close their eyes and raise their hands if they've ever said anything bad about another girl. Virtually every hand is raised. The reason this scene rings true is that it is true. And sadly, we are often even harder on ourselves.

In addition to the amazing news that Mary would bear God's son, the angel who visits her in Luke 1 also tells Mary of her goodness, of her favor in God's eyes. Mary was a teenage girl. Chances are, she'd heard—and thought—something less than kind about herself on more than one occasion. Consider her brave, beautiful response. Think of someone who loves you. What do they say about you? Decide today to let their words—and God's words—be the truth. Join Mary in saying to God, "May everything you have said about me come true."

Are you self-critical? If asked to describe yourself,
what would you say?

Resistance

Submit to one another
out of reverence for Christ.
EPHESIANS 5:21 NIV

In a world of equal opportunity and pursuit for equality, submission can be a tough pill to swallow. Perhaps there are just too many hang-ups with that word in English. If submission seems like a stumbling block to you, try thinking about the word acceptance.

The way the Scripture wants us to understand submission is perhaps best when thinking about its antonym. The opposite of submission is resistance, and this is where all sorts of trouble can brew. If you think of some recent arguments you may have had, you were probably resisting the idea, emotions, or actions of someone else. While you have equally valid ideas, emotions, and actions, lean into the love of Christ and learn to accept or relent once in a while, so his grace can be experienced through you.

In what ways have you been resisting something because of your own desires, and how might Christ be asking you to change?

Crafting Iron

Iron sharpens iron,
so one man sharpens another.
PROVERBS 27:17 NASB

In ancient times, crafting iron took a lot of time because there were no electric sharpening devices. It required dedication, persistence, and hard work. Friendships should aspire to offer the same level of commitment. By investing in our friendships and interacting in an honest way, we create the sort of relationships that allow us to speak into each other's lives and keep accountable.

A few surface-level conversations will not accomplish sharpening. Devotion to one another through thick and thin, honesty, and integrity are needed for us to help refine each other. We must be willing to speak truth, but also put in the tough work of walking with each other through the growing process.

How do you surround yourself with people you can rely on?
How can you be a reliable friend to others?

Passion for Life

Let my passion for life be restored,
tasting joy in every breakthrough you bring to me.
Hold me close to you with a willing spirit
that obeys whatever you say.

PSALM 51:12 TPT

In John 15:10-11, Jesus makes it clear that the joy we experience directly correlates with our obedience to God. Here, David is asking God to restore his passion and his joy. He had broken God's commandments to not commit adultery or murder. Now, he wishes to stay close to God so he can walk in obedience, joy, and restoration.

Disobedience causes turmoil and confusion. God's great love for us implemented commandments for us to follow. Only God can completely restore what has been broken. He is willing to forgive the most atrocious sins and restore us to himself. We must, however, be willing to obey him, turn away from our wrongdoings, and stay close to him with a willing spirit. Often we have to come to him for strength to willingly choose to do what is right.

What does it mean to have a willing spirit?

A Higher Vantage Point

Victory comes from you, O LORD.
May you bless your people.
PSALM 3:8 NLT

*I*n times of war, army strategists benefit from high vantage points. Looking upon the battlefield from above is the best way to formulate strategies for their troops. Before the use of satellite equipment and heat-sensing radar, views were limited to ground level, forcing strategists to use whatever maps and spies they could to predict enemy movement and position their men.

In the same way, our lives benefit from a higher viewpoint. When we rise above our circumstances and see life not from our own anxious, urgent, overwhelming perspective but from God's, life's battles become less intimidating as eternity's promises rise into view.

What does it look like for you to trust God in the battle today?
You can be confident that he will lead you safely to victory.

Seek His Face

Look to the LORD and his strength;
seek his face always.

1 CHRONICLES 16:11 NIV

*I*t can be difficult to ask for help at times, and we like to try to solve our problems on our own. That is not how the Lord created us to operate. We need his strength to persevere, and we need the support of others as well.

Rather than trying to muster up enough power to forge through life alone, we should seek the Lord's face and ask for help in times of trouble. The Lord is gracious and generous. He gives us strength, and he also gives us each other. When we feel overwhelmed and incapable of carrying on, we can come before to him and ask for strength.

Has the Lord put someone in your life who has been a source of strength and encouragement for you?

Mouth of Arrows

They sharpen their tongues like swords
and aim cruel words like deadly arrows.
PSALM 64:3 NIV

It can be difficult to ask for help at times, and we like to try to solve our problems on our own. That is not how the Lord created us to operate. We need his strength to persevere, and we need the support of others as well.

Rather than trying to muster up enough power to forge through life alone, we should seek the Lord's face and ask for help in times of trouble. The Lord is gracious and generous. He gives us strength, and he also gives us each other. We can thank him for his gift of communication and ask him to help us use our words for good and not harm.

How can you use your words to build others up today?

Compassionate

Be kind and compassionate to one another,
forgiving each other, just as in Christ God forgave you.
EPHESIANS 4:32 NIV

It is a well-known prospect that we become like those we associate with. Paul points out earlier in this chapter that traits which define worldly individuals are easily misled, possessing futile thinking, ignorant, hard of heart, insensitive, sensual, indulgent, impure, greedy, bitter, angry, prone to fight, and slanderous.

Instead, we are to be remade in the image of our Maker. He is kind, compassionate, and forgiving. This sort of behavior takes an intentional laying down of self, but it becomes more and more attainable when we spend intentional time with God.

Why do you think Paul so often writes about
the forgiveness we have received when he is
instructing us on how to treat others?

your Desires

Delight yourself in the LORD,
and he will give you the desires of your heart.
PSALM 37:4 ESV

It is hard to reconcile some of the promises in God's Word with our disappointment with things that we have asked for but haven't yet received. Perhaps you are waiting for an answer or are hoping for a miracle.

Be encouraged that Jesus says that we need to be persistent and resilient and that he is always willing to open the door to you so you can find him. When you allow Jesus into your life, you will receive all that you need. Ask for a resilient mind so you can keep asking, knocking, and seeking in faith that you will find what you need Put your trust in him, knowing that he cares for you and he will open the door to answer you when you knock.

*How is your faith encouraged by turning to Lord
at the beginning of the day?*

Calming Splashes

The raging waves lifted themselves over and over,
high above the ocean's depths, letting out their mighty roar!
Yet at the sound of your voice they were all stilled by your might.
What a majestic King, filled with power!
PSALM 93:4-5 TPT

Have you ever been so stressed that it almost felt like your body was vibrating? Your stomach flipped and flopped with nerves. Your cheeks were red. It's for sure your blood pressure was up. You didn't even need to check it to know that. And your last good nerve was on display so everyone could step on it…and they did.

Whoosh! Whooooosh! Whoosh! Gurgle. Whoosh! Whooooosh! Whoosh! Have you ever listened to the sound of water splashing on the rocks of a riverbank? You can almost feel the stress draining from your body as you enjoy God's handiwork. The soothing sound of the water eases the tension from your shoulders. We know that God can calm the waves, but he can also calm his children through the soothing sound of those waves.

Why do you think the sound of water is calming?
How do those waters reflect God's mighty power?

Weakness

That's why I take pleasure in my weaknesses, and in the insults,
hardships, persecutions, and troubles that I suffer for Christ.
For when I am weak, then I am strong.

2 CORINTHIANS 12:10 NLT

*I*t seems counterintuitive to boast about our weaknesses, but if God has ever intervened on our behalf and provided a way when we could not find our own, we should rejoice in it!

Our rejoicing can be multiplied when we share our story with others as well. In doing so, we boast of God in our weaknesses. When hardships come upon us, we have a unique opportunity to see how God will use them for our good and his glory. We can choose to view life differently than the world. We don't live for our own glory or selfish pursuits, so if God shows up during our troubles, we can welcome them and even rejoice in them!

When has God proven his strength through your weakness?

Share the Light

"It is too small a thing that You should be My Servant
To raise up the tribes of Jacob,
And to restore the preserved ones of Israel;
I will also give You as a light to the Gentiles,
That You should be My salvation to the ends of the earth."

ISAIAH 49:6 NKJV

It was always part of God's plan to bring salvation to his entire creation. We know the people of Israel are the chosen ones through whom God brought salvation, but we need to remember that God wanted his message to go to the ends of the earth.

Jesus didn't confine his ministry to the Jewish people and believers of his day. He extended his ministry to the Gentiles and everyone "outside" the law of the Scribes and the Pharisees. God doesn't want us to keep him to ourselves. He wants us to be a light that shines for all to see so that salvation can reach the ends of the earth.

Are you willing to be a light for Christ today?

In Sunshine and Storm

When times are good, be happy;
but when times are bad, consider this:
God has made the one as well as the other.
Therefore, no one can discover
anything about their future.

ECCLESIASTES 7:14 NIV

It's easy to feel happy on a sunny day, when all is well, the birds are singing, and life is going along swimmingly. But what happens when waters are rougher, bad news comes, or the days feel just plain hard?

God wants us to feel gladness when times are good. He has made each and every day. We are called to rejoice in all of them whether good or bad. Happiness is determined by our circumstances, but true joy comes when we can find the silver linings, hidden in our darkest hours—when we can sing his praises no matter what. We don't know what the future holds for us here on earth, but we can find our delight in the knowledge that our eternity is set in beauty.

Is your happiness determined by your circumstance?
Pray that you will discover true joy in our Creator.
Ask him to give you a deep and abiding satisfaction
that goes beyond human understanding.

Perpetual Praise

I will extol the LORD at all times;
his praise will always be on my lips.
PSALM 34:1 NIV

*I*t's relatively easy to sing God's praises when all is going well in our lives: when he blesses us with something we asked for, when he heals us, or when he directly answers a prayer. We naturally turn and give him praise and glory for good things. What about when things aren't going well? What about in dry times, painful times, or times of waiting?

Choose today to have praise readily on your lips instead of complaint. Whenever you feel discontentment or frustration, replace it with praise. By focusing on the goodness of God, the hardships will lessen and your joy will increase.

How can you choose praise even when your day has barely started and you can already feel the stresses mounting? How can you choose to be grateful instead of complaining?

My Fortress

The LORD is my light and my salvation—
so why should I be afraid?
The LORD is my fortress,
protecting me from danger,
so why should I tremble?

PSALM 27:1 NLT

It's time to face another day, and even though you might not feel ready for it, God is already strengthening you with peace, wisdom, and hope. Remember that you can always count on him to equip you with what you need as you need it.

What do you need right now? Is it motivation to simply have a shower and get dressed? Is it peace to calm your anxious nerves about an exam at school? You might need a bit of patience as you try and chase your kids to get ready for school. Ask him for what you need—he cares about the small stuff and is more than ready to give you help.

How can you allow God to be your help today?

Grow your Gift

Don't minimize the powerful gift that operates in your life, for it was imparted to you by the laying on of hands of the elders and was activated through the prophecy they spoke over you. Make all of this your constant meditation and make it real with your life so everyone can see that you are moving forward.

1 TIMOTHY 4:14-15 TPT

Jesus gave you special gifts and talents. It is as though he has a garden full of the most beautiful flowers, and if you do not rise and bloom, nothing will take your place.

This is exactly what is happening in the spiritual realm. If God had two of you, one would be redundant. Enjoy your life, your uniqueness, and your opportunities to bloom where you are planted, or be transplanted into a new pot to be enjoyed elsewhere. God has good things for you. God made you his flower and you are cherished as such. Bloom!

Where are you planted right now? How might you bloom?

Grief and Joy

"You too have grief now;
but I will see you again, and your heart will rejoice,
and no one will take your joy away from you."
JOHN 16:22 NASB

Jesus told his disciples of the sorrow they were about to bear at his crucifixion. Those around them would rejoice and they would mourn. They were not to be surprised or dismayed by this because they would surely see Jesus again.

Although death and sin rob from us now and inflict us with grief, they cannot withhold our joy. A day is coming when all will be restored, when the Lord will enact his final judgement and Jesus Christ will return for us. Since we have an eternal, Biblical mindset, there are instances when we grieve and the world around us celebrates. What is right and what is wrong seem to be mixed up. This will not last. One day, Jesus will turn the tables and our sorrow will be transformed into joy that nothing can destroy.

What do you rejoice over that the world scoffs at?
What grieves you that the world promotes?

Winter to Spring

"Let us acknowledge the Lord;
let us press on to acknowledge him.
As surely as the sun rises, he will appear;
he will come to us like the winter rains,
like the spring rains that water the earth."

HOSEA 6:3 NIV

Spring sometimes teases us. A few balmy, sunny days awaken our senses to the freshness of spring air and promise the end of winter. We fall into bed after hours of sunshine and laughter, only to reawaken to a white blanket covering any evidence of warmth. Spring sun hides behind winter clouds, teasing us as though they know of our longing for the great light they hide. When the sun finally re-emerges, we are bathed in instant warmth.

Our lives have winters, don't they? We live through seasons where we feel cold, hidden, and trapped. We feel buried under the snow of circumstance with an absence of clarity, warmth, and light. But, if we looked closer, perhaps we could see the rushing of the clouds, the gilded outlines that promise there is hope just past them. And though winter can be long, the moment when the sun returns will be worth it all.

Are you in the middle of one of life's winters?

yet to Come

He will yet fill your mouth with laughter
and your lips with shouts of joy.
JOB 8:21 NIV

Joy is the most natural thing when you are experiencing something exciting, fun, humorous, or satisfying. But the Scripture today comes from the book of Job, and if you know anything about this guy you will know that he was possibly feeling the most miserable anyone could feel. Job went through incredible pain: physically, mentally, spiritually, and emotionally.

How is it that this book of the Bible assures us that God fills us with laughter and shouts of joy? The clue could be in the word "yet." We may not be in a situation that feels very joyful; yet, there is hope of a day coming when we will once again laugh and shout with joy. If your world feels like that right now, hold on to the "yet." During those days when you feel apathetic, sad, or downright depressed, choose to look ahead to a day where your mouth will laugh and shout with joy. Be filled with the assurance that joy is waiting for you.

What do you see that is yet to come for you?
What hopes do you have for a brighter tomorrow?

Watch and See

Be still before the LORD
and wait patiently for him;
do not fret when people succeed in their ways,
when they carry out their wicked schemes.
PSALM 37:7 NIV

*J*ust when the Israelites thought they could catch their breath, Pharaoh reneged on his promise to let God's enslaved people go. He gathered the troops for a mighty pursuit. The Israelites were terrified. Ahead lay the impassable Red Sea and behind lay the formidable Egyptian army. Talk about stress. But God. The water that threatened to destroy the Israelites in the beginning served as a wall of protection and then a means to defeat evil. It was a miracle that only the Almighty God in heaven could perform.

When we feel like we're surrounded by enemies on all sides, when we struggle to overcome difficulties surrounding us, when we feel like this world is going to take us down, we need not worry, for our heavenly Father will fight for us. The battle is his. God still performs miracles. Despite our worries and anxieties, let's step out in faith and obedience even when trouble surrounds. Then let's watch and see what God will do.

What assurance do you have that God is with you always?

Seek Advice

Without counsel plans fail,
but with many advisers they succeed.
PROVERBS 15:22 ESV

Life is made up of decisions. Some are big, life altering decisions, and some are small. Should we go to college, choose this or that as a profession, move to Milwaukie? Should we plant a garden, buy a house, live in an apartment, take that seminar, or go to coffee with a friend? What about becoming a vegetarian, putting money into savings, or adopting a pet? Some of our choices may not require much more than common sense. Eating sushi or meatballs is pretty much up to personal preference but big decisions require more.

Before you buy a car, you should research what you can afford to spend, new or used, is it reliable or can you fix most problems? You should find out what other owners think of the car. Is it a lemon? Does it get good gas mileage? What will it cost to insure? God has instructed us to research, to investigate, and to plan. A wise person will take this advice for the important decisions in life. God doesn't want you to fail. He wants to bless you and help you prosper.

Do you have some big choices in your near future?
Are there people you trust that you can ask to help you?

Wide Awake

The one who watches over you
will not slumber.

PSALM 121:3 NLT

*L*ights dimmed the hospital corridors. Machines whirred, stopping
and starting. Now and then, the beep of an alarm sounded. Nurses
hurried in and out of patients' rooms without a sound. A mother
sat next to a metal-framed hospital bed, her head bent, shoulders
heaved as gulping sobs wrenched from her soul. She held her
daughter's hand covered with tape and tubes. After months of
bedside grief, she didn't want to sleep. Even though every fiber asked
for it. If she slept, in the morning her daughter might be gone.

There are times in our lives when we desperately need sleep but
dread it. Our hearts fear what dawn might bring, and our minds
cannot imagine the heart's upheaval a sunrise might present. So, we
force our eyelids awake, knowing beyond our night there might be
life in another form. We fear what tomorrow's morning might bring.
We agonize that we may need to learn to live again in a different way
with sorrow's companionship. When the morning light filters in, we
remind ourselves of this verse and know that God has not slept. He
has been watching over us through the night.

What brings sleep and peace to you in times of fear?

Love Covers

Above all, love each other deeply,
because love covers over a multitude of sins.
1 PETER 4:8 NIV

Love is what sets us apart from the world. We identify with Jesus because of love. Often love is not earned or deserved; it is given. Love can be very difficult and require all our strength. In fact, the type of love Peter is defining here as deep comes from the Greek word ektene, which was a term used to define an athlete's muscles when they were being strained to win a race. With this same determination, we are to love each other deeply above all else.

When we love others deeply, there is no room for sin to fester and cause bitterness. We can forgive sins, focus forward, mend relationships, and leave injustice in the capable hands of Christ. This is not easy, but with love it is possible. The love God shows us stands as a direct contrast to the love media and the world tries to sell. It is a love that is not tainted by sin. We can choose to cover sin with love, as God does for us.

Is there someone in your life you are striving to love?
Is unforgiveness or bitterness impeding you?

Musical Expression

Be filled with the Spirit, speaking to one another with psalms, hymns, and
songs from the Spirit. Sing and make music from your heart to the Lord.
EPHESIANS 5:18-19 NIV

Memory is a fascinating part of our brains. We have memories
triggered by specific smells, like freshly washed laundry, or tastes,
like an ice cream cone. Many memories are activated by music.
Songs can make or break a moment and stick in your head with
relentless tenacity. As powerful as music is, we often shy away from
using it as a tool. God wants us to participate in musical expression.
Maybe he is nudging you to spend your commute time listening to
worship instead of talk radio.

The beautiful thing is the song can hold the words of encouragement
that you need. A worship song can also cause you to remember a
friend in need and draw you into prayer for them. Don't shy away
from expressing yourself in music from your heart. Fill your life with
songs that point your eyes upward, and let music lead you to fight
for others in prayer.

What songs have been on your heart and mind lately?

Take the Leap

The LORD is my strength and my shield;
my heart trusts in him, and he helps me.
My heart leaps for joy, and with my song I praise him.
PSALM 28:7 NIV

Most great things in life take some risk. We probably can each say that we've taken some pretty dumb chances in life, but we have also taken some incredible ones. Some of our risks end in disaster, but others in sheer beauty.

One thing all risk has in common is that it teaches us something. We never walk away unchanged. And while stepping out and taking the risk itself is scary, we discover our own bravery in it. You can take measured risks with the Lord, knowing that he wants you to live a life of adventure. When he asks you to step out, you know it will be a risk worth taking.

How can you take a leap of faith today?

In Charge

"I am not even worthy to come and meet you.
Just say the word from where you are,
and my servant will be healed."

LUKE 7:7 NLT

Most of us like to think we're in control of situations. We often think we are more relaxed when we're in control. But no matter how good it feels to be in charge, there are times when we are relieved to give it up. We realize how much we can't control. Nothing brings that into reality as forcefully as sickness—ours—or someone we love. In the same way the centurion gave orders and was obeyed, he believed Jesus' authority could cure his servant's illness. He understood the power of Jesus' command.

We often spin our wheels trying to make things turn out the way we think they should. If you have been labeled a control freak, you know how hard it is to let go. Relinquishing control can be gut-wrenching. But it can also be a huge relief and a giant leap toward rest. Authority is an amazing thing. When we try to manage life on our own, it becomes a heavy burden. If we find rest illusive and sleep impossible, we need to check who's in control. When we submit to Jesus, it takes the weighty yoke of control from us.

What do you find difficult to submit to Jesus' authority?

Wherever I Go

If I fly with wings into the shining dawn, you're there!
If I fly into the radiant sunset, you're there waiting.

PSALM 139:9 TPT

Moving on from anywhere can be disconcerting. A new circumstance, house, or even country means that we have to leave what we have been comfortable with and step out into the unknown. Take courage that no matter where you go, the Lord will always go with you. He is as far east as the rising sun, and as far west as the sunset. He will guide you as you move, and he will hold you when you get there.

The world is small in comparison to God's presence. He promises to be with us wherever we go. He will guide the next steps of your life and give you the confidence to move on to where he has called you. You can trust him from the rising of the sun to its setting.

When do you most sense God's presence with you?

April

"Do not be grieved,
for the joy of the LORD
is your strength."

NEHEMIAH 8:10 ESV

Rest Secure

I keep my eyes always on the LORD.
With him at my right hand, I will not be shaken.
Therefore my heart is glad and my tongue rejoices;
my body also will rest secure.
PSALM 16:8-9 NIV

No matter where you are, God is there also. While there may be times when we ache to hide from him in our shame, he is a constant presence. The beautiful thing about his omnipresence is that we have a steady and consistent companion who is always ready to help in times of trouble.

We have no reason to fear the things that the world may throw our way. We've got the best protector of all at our side! Are you asking for his help in times of worry and woe, or are you turning inward to try to solve your problems? Let God be your refuge. Nothing is too big or too small for him. Even in your darkest hours, you can know true joy because he is your guardian.

How can you take your cares and distress, and cast them on God? Do you know that he can handle them?

Set Apart

"Before you were born I set you apart."
JEREMIAH 1:5 NIV

Nobody was an accident or an afterthought. The Lord has carefully crafted every person uniquely. He loved each of us before we were even born because he planned in his heart and mind exactly how we were meant to be.

Sometimes we try to deviate away from how the Lord created us and the calling he has placed on our lives, but as we search for peace to accept who we are and how we were formed, we can have confidence that the Lord truly knows us. He knew us before the world began to hurt and influence us, and he knows how to restore us as well.

How are you set apart?

Different Gifts

In his grace, God has given us different gifts for doing certain things well.
So if God has given you the ability to prophesy,
speak out with as much faith as God has given you.

ROMANS 12:6 NLT

Of what benefit is it if someone were to give a child a gift, but that child never opened it or used it? God has given each of us natural abilities, talents, and spiritual gifts. He wants to teach us how to use them and what they are for. With the faith that we have, he asks us to step out in our gifts. In time our faith will grow.

Imagine if the child who received the gift only wanted to play by himself. God's great plans for giving gifts includes serving and encouraging the entire body of believers. He has given each of us a special position in his family and the tools we need to play our part well. Our gifts are not for us alone but to be used to help others.

Do you have the faith to step out and use your gifts?
How can they bless others?

Chosen Ones

You are a chosen race, a royal priesthood, a holy nation, God's own people,
in order that you may proclaim the mighty acts of him who called you
out of darkness into his marvelous light.

1 PETER 2:9 NRSV

On occasion, we need a little nudge for all the pieces of our
disposition to fall into alignment with God's. Today's nudge is a
grand reminder of our identity as a Christian body. We are each holy
priests serving the Living God! He is risen, and we are singly and
corporately his. Because of this, we each walk in his light, and we
shepherd others into the light as well.

Sometimes, it is difficult to get rid of the grumpy feelings of the
day. It seems okay to have a lower opinion of ourselves and our
circumstances (and maybe other people). But the truth is that God's
opinion is our opinion, and we are to shout that in everything we
do. Priests carry a message to the people. What message are you
carrying today?

*How will you share the good news of
God's attitude toward others?*

A Genuine Love

Love each other with genuine affection
and take delight in honoring each other.

ROMANS 12:10 NLT

One of the most difficult things to do is to love someone who doesn't want to be loved. To love those who push you away every time you try to help, those who are difficult, and those who are maybe even a little mean is discouraging, defeating, even costly.

Genuine love keeps showing up. It continues to extend a hand of grace. It serves in every capacity possible. It sees the whole person. Sometimes the hardness of a person is just a mask. Often those difficult people need to know deep down inside that they are worth the effort.

Is there someone in your life that is difficult to love? Reach out to them today and let them know they are seen.

Written

A person may have many ideas concerning God's plan for his life,
but only the designs of his purpose will succeed in the end.
PROVERBS 19:21 TPT

Our futures, just like our pasts, are in the hands of God. We were not an afterthought or a disposable extra detail. In fact, we were created for a very specific part in God's family, and we are irreplaceable in the eyes of the Lord. He made each of us from the outpouring of his love, and by his design we came to be.

During the hard days we can remember that the Lord has a purpose for those as well. Every one of our days are known by God and destined for us even before our lives began. The point of the hard days is not to just move us to the good days. There are incredible lessons to be learned and insights to be gleaned from every day we are given.

What gives you joy and appreciation
for the difficult days in life?

Busyness

"Come away by yourselves to a secluded place and rest a while."
(For there were many people coming and going,
and they did not even have time to eat.)
MARK 6:31 NASB

Our lives are so full that we often have difficulty finding time to spend with Jesus. We have so much that demands our attention, it can be hard to find time to consecrate a portion of our day to God. He, who has existed for eternity, is not bound by time. Because he is outside of time, time does not limit him the way that it limits us. When we take even a few sacred minutes to spend in his presence in the midst of our busy day, he can meet us there and download deep truths to our hearts.

In the days when you feel you don't even have time to eat, ask God to give you the grace to find a few moments to slip away alone in his presence. God will speak volumes to a heart that is open to his truth—even over the hustle and bustle of your busiest days.

How can you open your heart to God's truth
even in your busy moments?

Heart Truth

O Lord, who shall sojourn in your tent?
Who shall dwell on your holy hill?
He who walks blamelessly and does what is right
and speaks truth in his heart.

PSALM 15:1-2 ESV

Our thoughts need coaching because most of the time they will derail. It is natural to become self-focused throughout the day. In doing so, insecurities and fears can subconsciously be strengthened. It's important to pause throughout the day and take stock in what we have given our minds to.

There is great value in actively controlling your mind. It is critical to speak the truth to our hearts. Don't be discouraged when you see that you aren't walking closely with God. View it as a revelation from God to help you correct your course. He will give you the strength you need to align your mind with his truth.

Are you speaking truth in and to your heart?

Walk Wisely

Be very careful, then, how you live—
not as unwise but as wise,
making the most of every opportunity,
because the days are evil.

EPHESIANS 5:15-16 NIV

*P*aul had been beaten, shipwrecked, stoned, imprisoned, and homeless. He was well aware that any day could be his last. Although we may not have been beckoned by death as often as he, we also do not know when our lives will end.

Our time on earth is not just short, it is filled with evil days as well. Everywhere we look, unwise people live for themselves and reject the grace of God. Our lives should be led by the wisdom that comes from God so we can be pleasing to him and an example to others. When we live like this, we can make the most of every opportunity to witness to others.

How do you walk in wisdom?

Accept your Gift

Do not neglect the gift that is in you, which was given to you by prophecy
with the laying on of the hands of the eldership. Meditate on these things;
give yourself entirely to them, that your progress may be evident to all.

1 Timothy 4:14-15 nkjv

Paul wrote to Timothy, encouraging him to use his gift of teaching.
Of what profit is it to simply possess gifts if we forgo using them?
God has invested a unique set of traits in each of us to reflect himself
and to play an intrinsic part in his plan.

God will teach us how to use our gifts and offer us opportunities to
put them to use if we trust his leading and guiding. It is important
that we refrain from becoming jealous of someone else's gift and
praise God for the gifts he has given to us, learning to use them for
his glory.

How can you learn to use your gifts wisely?

Poverty

One who is gracious to a poor man lends to the LORD,
and He will repay him for his good deed.

PROVERBS 19:17 NASB

People can be poor in many ways. In our environment, we may not come across true poverty or see homeless people in our day-to-day lives. But there are those who suffer from poverty of joy, hope, and love. There are those around you, even today, who are hurting from their lack of being loved by someone or suffering from despair.

Ask the Holy Spirit to show you those who are poor in spirit and find a way to bring grace into their situation. It might be practical help, a kind word, or an invitation out for coffee. Let the grace that dwells in you be poured out on those around you and know that your heavenly Father will be overjoyed that you are sharing his love.

In what ways and forms have you seen poverty in the people around you? Consider the ways that you can lend to the poor.

Floodwaters

The LORD rules over the floodwaters.
The LORD reigns as king forever.
PSALM 29:10 NLT

Picture a season in your life where you were knee-deep in busyness, swallowed in sadness, or buried in exhaustion. Picture that season and how you looked, acted, reacted, and survived.

Now picture the King of the heavens and earth. See how he rules over the entire earth. This powerful God wants you to lean on him, and that seems easy to do when you understand just how great and mighty he is. If you have woken up feeling tired, lean on the strength of your Savior.

Do you feel weary and weak? How can you rely on God to be your source of power today?

Cheerful Face

A joyful heart makes a cheerful face,
but when the heart is sad, the spirit is broken.

PROVERBS 15:13 NASB

Real joy is lasting and is not deterred by circumstances here on earth, for it is caused by the hope we have in Jesus for our eternity. Since it is secured in that which will not fail, it cannot be broken by anything we know to be momentary. Our joy is a gift that cannot be taken away. It helps us to find cheer when everything in our lives seems to be in disarray.

There will be times of sadness in all our lives. Each one of us will face our own tragedies. It is when we give way to sadness and allow it to dictate our condition that our spirit is broken and we can no longer find the motivation to press forward. With eternity in our hearts, we must cling to the joy that has been given to us. It will give us the strength and determination we need to overcome.

What is the difference between having joy and feeling happy?

Slaying the Giants

David said to the Philistine, "You come against me with sword and spear and javelin, but I come against you in the name of the LORD Almighty, the God of the armies of Israel, whom you have defied. This day the LORD will deliver you into my hands."

1 SAMUEL 17:45-46 NIV

*R*emember the Bible story of the shepherd boy, David, and the Philistine giant, Goliath? Goliath had been taunting the Israelites for forty days, daring someone to come fight him. To say that the Israelites were stressed was an understatement. Goliath was huge and terrifying, and nobody was brave enough to fight him except that shepherd boy who gathered five smooth stones from the stream.

We all have giants in our lives. Our giants are real and they can rock our world, stressing us to the limit. In those moments, we need to remember what that shepherd boy did: he was going to face the giant armed with God. That's where our power lies. Giants stress us, but God fights our battles. The next time you're weighed down with stress over situations that you can't fix, go to the one who can. Then go out with his strength and watch as he conquers the situations that stress and worry you.

What do you think gave David the courage to stand up to the giant when others didn't?

A New Creation

If anyone is in Christ, he is a new creation.
The old has passed away; behold, the new has come.
2 CORINTHIANS 5:17 ESV

Sarah's pajamas didn't feature images of playful kittens, stylish shoes, or mugs of hot cocoa with cute sayings. Her mattress wasn't six inches thick with cushy memory foam on top. She didn't kiss her loved ones good-night and then ease into sleep with soft music playing in the background. Sarah's pajamas were prison-issued. Her mattress was thin, the cell cheerless, and she was far from loved ones, both in distance and relationship. In her wildest dreams, she would never have imagined herself in this cell.

Every night when she stretched out to sleep, all she could see in the dark was the image of her mother's brokenhearted face. All she could hear was her tears. She hadn't been able to sleep well since her incarceration. It's hard to sleep when guilt and shame are crushing the breath from you. But then during a service at the prison, she heard the story of God's love. She learned about a God with grace and mercy, one who could make a new creation out of her messed-up life. Sarah asked Jesus into her heart that day, and for the first time in a long time, her sleep was sweet.

How does becoming a new creation provide sweet rest?

Little People

"The Son of Man came to seek and to save the lost."
LUKE 19:10 NIV

When our bodies are tired and our spirits match, it is easy to look at the great big world and feel very small. We try not to pay attention to numbers, but we do. We see how few likes we get on social media or watch promotions fly by to land on others. We wonder why we are spinning our wheels. Why are the big bucks heading in another direction? And sometimes it hits us.

I'm just a little person.

Little people have great value to Jesus. Sooner or later all of us look at the world and compare. The scope of our tiny place in a big world shrinks in our minds as insignificant, and we head to bed wondering if all the rush and hard work has any worth or purpose at all. Jesus came for all. He is our salvation and significance. Little people with a great God have a divine purpose. Think about that today.

What makes you feel insignificant, and how does that affect your rest? How do God's purposes change those thoughts?

Refuge and Strength

God is our refuge and strength,
always ready to help in times of trouble.
So we will not fear when earthquakes come
and the mountains crumble into the sea.

PSALM 46:1-2 NLT

Since we have an eternal perspective and we know that God is our help in times of trouble, we can have confidence rather than fear when disaster strikes. When others are overcome with worry or doubt, we continue to focus on God and trust his hand will guide us.

Our strength and our courage come from God. Even if everything is crumbling down around us, we can find refuge in him because he is greater than the world. He is always prepared to offer his people comfort and hope in times of tragedy. We can ask for his understanding to transform our wordly mindsets. We do not need to worry about the future like those who rely on themselves. We don't seek shelter behind temporary shields because God is our covering. We don't cower in the face of danger like those whose only defense is themselves. God is our refuge and strength.

What is your initial reaction when catastrophe hits?

Sleep Like a King

That night the king could not sleep;
so he ordered the book of the chronicles,
the record of his reign,
to be brought in and read to him.
ESTHER 6:1 NIV

Some nights we collapse into bed. Other nights it's a long, delicious process of winding down and letting the day's busyness melt away. You may have a bedtime routine which helps you relax—a book, a hot bath, or a nice cup of chamomile tea. Most of us would not choose King Xerxes' strategy in the book of Esther, however the sheer boredom of reading records would likely put any of us to sleep.

God uses even sleepless nights for his purposes. Can it be God has your eyes open and mind alert for an unseen reason? Your reason may be as simple as prayer. Perhaps someone needs intercession and you are awake for that purpose. God used the king's sleepless night to express gratitude for a past blessing. But ultimately his insomnia humiliated God's enemies and saved a nation. His tedium of lists and events proved to be part of a much greater plan.

Do you sometimes waken with someone on your mind who you think needs prayer? What do you do?

Vulnerability

He gives us more grace. That is why Scripture says:
"God opposes the proud
but shows favor to the humble."

JAMES 4:6 NIV

Some of the most substantial and ultimately wonderful changes in our lives come from moments of vulnerability: laying our cards on the table, so to speak, and letting someone else know how much they really mean to us. But vulnerability takes one key ingredient: humility. And humility is not an easy pill to swallow. Isn't it sometimes easier for us to pretend that conflict never happened than to face the fact that we made a mistake and wronged another person? It's not always easy to humble ourselves and fight for the resolution in an argument—especially when it means admitting our failures.

Who are you in the face of conflict? Do you avoid apologizing in an attempt to save face? Does your pride get in the way of vulnerability, or are you willing and ready to humble yourself for restoration in your relationships? God says that he will give favor and wisdom to the humble.

What can you do today to humble yourself
for the sake of a restored relationship?

Faith or Sight

We are always confident and know that as long as we are at home in the body we are away from the Lord. For we live by faith, not by sight.

2 CORINTHIANS 5:6-7 NIV

Sometimes we demand a lot of God. "God, I'd like this house," "God, this is my dream job," "I'm so ready to have a husband," and we wait in expectation. We wait for him to do the impossible. We wait for him to give us the desires of our hearts. Because if he does, then he is most definitely all-powerful. If he does, he heard your cry and answered. If he does, he loves you. This is living by sight.

In 2 Corinthians it says we live by faith, not sight. We often doubt God. Living by faith is giving up any control we thought we had, and sitting in the passenger seat in eager anticipation of where God is taking us.

Have you been living by faith or by sight? How can you let go of unfulfilled desires, and start living by faith? God's desires for you are great! He wants only the best for you and asks for your faith in return.

Unexpected Angels

The LORD hears good people when they cry out to him,
and he saves them from all their troubles.
PSALM 34:17 NCV

Sometimes your rescue can come in the form of another person. We cry out to God and ask him for help, but we shouldn't presume to know exactly how he is going to help us. God has humanity in his image and can express himself through people with their kind acts, words of encouragement, and often a great piece of advice or wisdom.

Thank God today for the people that he has put in your life and the unexpected ways that he can use them to encourage you. Thank him for revealing himself to you through others. Thank him that you can be part of the healing and grace he longs to share with the broken world.

What are you crying out to God for right now?
Could he be answering you through someone else?

Showers of Blessings

"Fear not, for I am with you;
be not dismayed, for I am your God;
I will strengthen you, I will help you,
I will uphold you with my righteous right hand."

ISAIAH 41:10 ESV

Jill's newborn son, Adam, was beautiful. But as the months went by, he started missing milestones that babies are supposed to reach at various ages. It soon became clear Adam would never talk, sit up, or walk. More children joined their family. Children with no health issues. Jill loved them all, with a tender love for the little son who required extra care. Her heart and days were full. She didn't begrudge a minute of all the care she gave, but she was beyond exhausted.

Many women would have folded under all the stress and physical demands. But not Jill. You see, Jill had discovered the best place to get the strength she needed. She listened to an audio Bible, the promises from God's Word soaking into her weary soul. She prayed as she folded laundry. And she played praise and worship music. The precious words of the songs showered her with blessings as they told about God's power and comfort, and how he's always with us.

How can you discover showers of blessings in trying moments?

Tears on My Pillow

Weeping may tarry for the night,
but joy comes with the morning.
PSALM 30:5 ESV

Still half-asleep, Rose reached over in the darkness to put her arm around her husband…and felt nothing but emptiness. She jerked awake, raw grief overwhelming her as tears soaked into her pillowcase. He wasn't there anymore. He never would be again. Rose knew Rob was with Jesus now, that he was in a better place, but that didn't lessen the pain of her sweetheart being gone.

Perhaps you're like Rose. You've lost a sweetheart or someone close to you. Perhaps your grief is so deep that it's hard to catch your breath. You wonder if you'll ever smile again or how you'll make it through the weeks and months ahead. But you will. Cling to Jesus. His love will ease the pain like nothing else can. Yes, life will be different, but the sun will shine again. You will smile, and you will laugh again. God will not leave you comfortless, and he will be enough for all that you're going through. As he has promised, he will give you rest—sweet rest—and joy will come in the morning. Tried and proven.

What can you do when grief overwhelms you? What promises from God's Word can you claim as your personal promises?

Healthy Trees

Like trees planted in the Temple of the LORD,
they will grow strong in the courtyards of our God.
PSALM 92:13 NCV

Take a moment to reflect on a time when you felt you were giving the best of yourself. You may be thinking of times when you were utilizing your gifts and talents and could witness your positive influence in others around you. You may not have to reflect back far, or you could be wondering where those times have gone!

Jesus describes himself as the vine. If we are being nourished from that source, we will produce fruit. In the times where we feel like we are not flourishing, it may be that the Father needs to do some necessary pruning—for the health of both the branch and the whole vine.

Which areas of your life do you feel God has chosen to prune?
How can you be encouraged that God is doing this so you can
be fruitful in other areas of your life?

Approach God

In him and through faith in him we may approach God
with freedom and confidence.
EPHESIANS 3:12 NIV

The access we have to approach God in prayer comes from Christ's sacrifice for our sins. We have been made pure and clean, so we can freely approach him. The confidence we have to come before him is because of our faith in Christ's sacrifice for us. He died for us, purified us, established our faith, and invited us to approach God.

None of what God did for us was by our merit, it is our free gift of salvation and means we have relationship with our Savior. We can only choose to respond and embrace it. As you come before him in prayer, recognize that even the right to approach God is a gift from him. Thank him for breaking down the divide between you and him. Praise him for the freedom and confidence he has filled you with. Remember how blessed you are to serve a God who desires relationship with his creation.

Do you have confidence in Christ? How do you know?

Mindset of Christ

In your relationships with one another, have the same mindset as Christ
Jesus: Who, being in very nature God, did not consider equality with God
something to be used to his own advantage and being found in appearance
as a man, he humbled himself by becoming obedient to death—
even death on a cross!
PHILIPPIANS 2:5-6, 8 NIV

The attitude Christ bore was one of servanthood and sacrifice. His humble obedience is meant to serve as a model for us to replicate. If the King of the universe is willing to overlook his grandiose rights for the sake of love, and subject himself to all the mistreatment of the world, then we can also partake in serving others in the relationships God has given us.

Whatever our current calling, we know we are walking with a God who understands. He can help you embrace the relationships he has given you with the same attitude he has for others. You can love others the way he has loved you when you do it through his strength.

As you find yourself in situations that require Christlike servanthood, do you embrace them with a humble and obedient mindset as well?

Compassion and Justice

The LORD longs to be gracious to you;
therefore he will rise up to show you compassion.
For the LORD is a God of justice.
Blessed are all who wait for him!
ISAIAH 30:18 NIV

The beautiful blending of God's compassion and justice is what gives us the hope that he will amend everything in his timing. We long for his justice now, but he compassionately holds back his judgment a while longer.

This same compassion forgave our sins and showed us grace when we were worthy of death. God's amazing grace lifts us back up. We wait patiently for the Lord because we know his grace is abounding and his fairness is exact.

How has God shown you grace?

Miraculous

You are the God who does miracles;
you have shown people your power.

PSALM 77:14 NCV

The Bible is full of exciting accounts of power, healing, and resurrection. We find ourselves wishing that we had been there when the fire of God fell upon Elijah's sacrifice, or when the storm was stilled by a voice, or when the blind man gained sight, or when Lazarus stepped out of the tomb.

God is clear that miracles didn't stop when the Bible ended. His power isn't limited by the ages, and he is just as omnipotent today as he always has been. Approach this day with hope in your heart. God is a God of the impossible.

Do you have faith to believe in the miracles that God did in the Bible and to believe that he can do miracles today?

True Life

This is how God showed his love to us:
He sent his one and only Son into the world
so that we could have life through him.

1 JOHN 4:9 NCV

The Bible is so clear that Jesus is God's Son and that true life is found only through him. It says that God sent him, implying that he came here from elsewhere. Jesus was not simply born here like the rest of us; he existed before time with God and as God. They are one together and divine in nature.

Being sent also indicates that Jesus had been given a mission. He was not on a casual visit to earth, but on an assignment to demonstrate God's love for us, his complete dominance over death and all evil realms, and to free us from every form of bondage by taking it on himself.

How does this verse remind you that love is more than a feeling; it demonstrates actions and change?

Life in Christ

If there is any encouragement in Christ, any comfort in love, any
participation in the Spirit, any affection and sympathy, complete my joy by
being of the same mind, having the same love, being in full accord and of
one mind.

PHILIPPIANS 2:1-2 ESV

The cause and effect outlined in these verses speak to the relevance
of the love of Christ and, as consequence, Christian love. Christ is
our encouragement and his love comforts us. The Holy Spirit guides
us and is involved in our lives. Anyone who has accepted Christ as
their Savior is well acquainted with his affection and sympathy.

The next verse relates the clear outcome of such moralities: we
will experience joy, love, and have a similar mindset as other
believers which unites us under Christ. This letter was written to the
Philippians so long ago, and yet the same truths are evident in our
lives today. Praise God for being the completion of our love, joy,
and unity.

*If being in full accord and of one mind with other believers is a
natural result of the love of Christ, why is there division
in the church?*

May

"Do not fear, for I am with you;
do not be dismayed, for I am your God.
I will strengthen you and help you;
I will uphold you with my righteous right hand."

ISAIAH 41:10 NIV

Lulled to Sleep

A young man named Eutychus, sitting at the window,
sank into a deep sleep as Paul talked still longer.
ACTS 20:9 ESV

The church was filled with worshippers. A young father with his family found an empty row and settled down. Soft familiar music caressed the air. Soon their youngest slept, nestled into her mother's lap. The father yearned to give way to the waves of sleep drawing his eyelids down like weighted wool. The unwelcome grip of sleep is like torture. Being lulled to sleep at the wrong time can be downright dangerous too, as Eutychus discovered when the Apostle Paul talked until past midnight.

Eutychus' is a much more dramatic story of falling asleep during a sermon than the young man with his family at church, but all of us can relate. There is another type of being lulled to sleep that's even more dangerous. It's the kind that dulls our senses to spiritual things. By renewing and refreshing our spiritual lives, we find new calm. If you find yourself barely able to keep your eyes open when they should be, yet you toss and turn unable to sleep at night, perhaps it is a spiritual wake-up call. No matter the hour of the day or night, the words of God bring rest.

How can you be more aware of your spiritual alertness?

Ask and Receive

"Keep on asking, and you will receive what you ask for.
Keep on seeking, and you will find.
Keep on knocking, and the door will be opened to you."

MATTHEW 7:7 NLT

The disciples had obviously asked God for many things before Jesus uttered these words. However, Jesus had been with them on earth. He had not yet accomplished on the cross what he came to earth to do, he had not stood as mediator before God for us, the veil had not yet been torn, and the Holy Spirit had not been given to us.

Christ's death and resurrection provided the way for us to approach God once again because our sins had been forgiven. The Holy Spirit came to help guide us in the way we should go, and he reforms our minds to be one with Christ. When we pray and our hearts are aligned with what that of Jesus, God will surely give us everything we need and fill our joy.

What does it mean to ask in Jesus' name?

Encourage Others

Encourage one another and build one another up,
just as you are doing.
1 THESSALONIANS 5:11 NASB

The events of life and the digression of the world should not shock us or cause us to panic. Instead, the realization that one day we will go home to Jesus should encourage us and reassure us through the dismal times. We are called upon to share that encouragement with other believers so they too can be motivated to endure.

As we edify others, may it be with a heart that yearns to see them prosper in their life with the Lord. As each person is different, so how they become motivated will be different. We need to listen and learn from the Lord regarding his creations. Then, let us humbly serve other believers, provide them comfort, and spur them on in their faith.

How can you encourage someone else today?

Wonderfully Made

I praise you because I am fearfully and wonderfully made;
your works are wonderful, I know that full well.
PSALM 139:14 NIV

The Father created us in his image for his purpose with much care and consideration. We should be careful not to complain about the handiwork of God, but to praise him for his wonderful design. He is worthy of admiration not resentment and criticism.

Taking care of ourselves can be a way of respecting God for his gift but rejecting the wonderful way he made us by hating who we are is unappreciative. We should consider how the Lord delights in us and how he created us for his pleasure. Rather than comparing ourselves to others, we can ask for his eyes to see the way he does. We can revel in our unique and wonderful design while giving him all the glory and praise.

Do you seek to improve yourself out of contempt for the way
you were made or out of care for what God has given you?

Everlasting Love

"I have loved you with an everlasting love;
I have drawn you with unfailing kindness."
JEREMIAH 31:3 NIV

The Israelites often turned away from God in favor of other idols or of themselves. Then, when they faced persecution, they would run back to the Lord. Over and over, he received them back. He does not turn aside a contrite heart. True repentance should not present only when help is needed, but the Lord understood the weakness of the Israelites and continued to welcome them home, showing them unfailing kindness.

Even when your faith is weak, the Lord will accept you if you ask. He helps you to mature in faith and gives you ample amounts of grace. His love is everlasting and his compassion is certain. His mercy is undeniable. Thank him for forgiving your sins again and again, for calling you back to him, and for treating you as a true heir of his kingdom.

When you try to forge your own way, do you sense the Lord
drawing you back to himself?

The Lord's Delight

His pleasure is not in the strength of the horse,
nor his delight in the legs of the warrior;
the LORD delights in those who fear him,
who put their hope in his unfailing love.

PSALM 147:10-11 NIV

The Lord is not lacking in strength; our show of power does not impress him. He wants us to learn how to trust in him and rely on his might rather than attempt to muscle our way through life in our own strength. Humility is far more pleasing to the Lord than ability. Our skills and strength are gifts from God, and our humble love is our grateful gift back to him.

Both the mighty horse and the tender butterfly were created by God, both are cared for by God, and both reflect a side of his character. Even if we feel confident and capable, we ought to fear God and follow his leadership. This will be pleasing to the Lord and will keep us out of a lot of potential trouble.

How has God displayed both his strength
and his tenderness in your life?

Condemnation

"Do not judge others, and you will not be judged.
Do not condemn others, or it will all come back against you.
Forgive others, and you will be forgiven."

LUKE 6:37 NLT

The Lord requires his children to extend grace toward others, since he covered us with his grace. He judged us innocent because Christ paid for our sins. Yet, if we judge others, then we choose to relinquish God's forgiving verdict of us. As soon as we condemn others by holding them to their sins, we condemn ourselves and all our sins will be held against us.

To overlook God's command on how we should love one another is to decline God's love for us. His love is unchanging, but he will withhold his grace from those who withhold it from others. His Word is clear. The choice is ours.

Do you find it difficult not to judge others?
How does this verse help you with that?

Path of Life

The path of the righteous is like the morning sun,
shining ever brighter till the full light of day.
PROVERBS 4:18 NIV

The path to life can be treacherous at times. It often leads us places we do not like to go. However, there is joy found in the journey. Not only are there eternal pleasures stored up for those who remain faithful, but there are rewards here now for following God. The greatest of these rewards is that we grow closer to God the more we walk with him. We understand his love, his character, and his plan better because we have a relationship with him.

Following God is the only path that leads to true and lasting life. When we stay the course, he fills us with joy, makes his presence known, and leads us every step of the way.

What sort of eternal pleasures has God promised
to those who faithfully follow him?

Protection

Let all who take refuge in you be glad;
let them ever sing for joy.
Spread your protection over them,
that those who love your name may rejoice in you.

PSALM 5:11 NIV

The remarkable grace God gives us provides impenetrable protection and insatiable joy! Since we love the Lord so much, his protection makes us glad and we rejoice in it. If we did not understand God, we would likely not appreciate his protection. We would fight against his laws and act out in disobedience. Then, we would also be vulnerable to all the enemy's attacks and all the elements of the world.

The Lord's protection does not guarantee that we will be spared from pain or sadness. It is a safety much more lasting, protecting our hearts from failing and keeping our feet on the path that leads to life. Those who do not understand will attempt to build their own barricade, but for those of us who realize what God's grace entails, we have every reason to rejoice.

How can you show appreciation to God
for his protection over you?

The Great Escape

The LORD brought his people out of Egypt,
loaded with silver and gold;
and not one among the tribes of Israel even stumbled.
PSALM 105:37 NLT

The story of Israel's rescue from hundreds of years of slavery in Egypt is not to be thought of lightly. What a miracle that God's chosen people were finally delivered. There were generations after generations that were born and died in slavery, and finally this was the generation that God set free. Not only were they set free, but he loaded them with silver and gold and made it easy for them to escape.

Sometimes these stories seem so far away in history that we don't relate to them. We need oto remind ourselves that God is the God of yesterday, today, and forever. He is as present this day as he was with his people hundreds of years ago. What a powerful God we serve!

What do you need God to help you escape from today?

In His Arms

And He took them in His arms and began blessing them,
laying His hands on them.

MARK 10:16 NASB

The term blessing here comes from the Greek word eulogeo, which means either to celebrate or to consecrate. Whether we are parents or we take care of other children, we recognize that there is no way for us to perfectly protect and provide for them alone. Only God has true power and authority over their lives, so we have to consecrate them to him and trust that he cares for them even more than we can.

Jesus lived by example, and he has asked us to follow in his steps. He prioritized children, celebrated them, and even used them in his mission. Children are not a burden to Jesus but a blessing that he embraces. We can trust him with the children in our lives.

How can you value the life of a child today?

Sweet Dreams

Fully awake, he rebuked the storm and shouted to the sea, "Hush!
Calm down!" All at once the wind stopped howling and the water
became perfectly calm.

MARK 4:39 TPT

The wind picked up and seemed to come from all directions.
The boat began to rock side to side and pitch forward and back.
Lightening lit the pitch-black sky, thunder rumbled, and rain pelted.
The disciples should've been sleeping. It had been a stressful day of
ministry by the lake with Jesus. Yet the disciples couldn't sleep, not
with the storm raging all around them. In fact, they were so anxious
about the weather that they actually thought they might lose their
lives that night.

Stressful situations and events can cause temporary insomnia. The
disciples worried about a violent storm and couldn't close their eyes.
We can also worry about storms in our lives. Sleep is important to
our bodies for obvious reasons, but lack of sleep can create anxiety,
and anxiety can lead to lack of sleep, so we need to be careful not to
fall into a vicious cycle. Troubles may surround us, but Jesus never
leaves us nor forsakes us. He can calm our hearts and allay our fears.
God is completely aware of the storms of life that trouble us.

Why do you still worry when Jesus is with you?

Look Up

Let us run with endurance
the race God has set before us.
HEBREWS 12:1 NLT

The writer of Hebrews compares our Christian journey to that of running a race. When we run a race, particularly a long one, we need perseverance to not quit when it gets hard. Races often start out feeling quite manageable, but inevitably there comes a point when completing the race seems not only daunting but perhaps impossible.

When this happens, it seems like the runner's eyes lower to the ground and rest on the monotony of watching one foot after the other slowly propel them forward. When you watch the ground while running, your distance gained is almost imperceptible. However, when you look up, toward your goal, you become reinvigorated to endure and persist. Your call as a runner is to fix your eyes on God. If you watch the ground or look behind you, you'll grow weary. But eyes staid on him will give you all the strength you need.

Do you stare at your discouraging circumstances more than at Jesus?

Burning the Candle

It is in vain that you rise up early and go late to rest,
eating the bread of anxious toil;
for he gives to his beloved sleep.

PSALM 4:8 NIV

There are days where you might wake up a little more sluggish, with a little less energy and positivity about the day. That can feel kind of empty, a gap you're hoping to fill.

The great thing about the God you serve is that in him you can be complete. He can be the gap filler. As you sit with him, his light begins to burn brighter. When it's hard to get out of bed because you feel anxious or worried about the day ahead, ask God for the energy and strength to face another day. He will give you what you need.

What does your schedule look like right now? Are you burning the candle at both ends, or do you allow time for rest and connection with God?

Well Timed

Everyone enjoys giving great advice.
But how delightful it is to say the right thing at the right time!
PROVERBS 15:23 TPT

There are situations in life where you feel lost for words. Often this is in moments of deep grief, sudden shock, or extreme surprise. Overwhelming emotions can be hard to express and when someone shares these emotions with us, we don't always know how to reply. The Bible speaks a lot about being slow to speak, so God doesn't expect us to know what to say immediately.

An appropriate response to someone doesn't have to be quick, it's just good if it's timely. The next time you find yourself lost for words, give yourself time to think and pray about a response. There's wisdom in letting the Holy Spirit guide you with encouraging words. Think of the joy you can bring to someone, perhaps not instantly, but in time, with the right words.

When was the last time you felt like you weren't able to give an appropriate reply? Ask God to give you some encouraging words for that person—perhaps now is the right time for them to hear it!

Peaceful Sleep

I lie down and sleep;
I wake again, because the LORD sustains me.
PSALM 3:3-4 NIV

There is always something to worry about, isn't there? Whether it's health, finances, relationships, or details, there are many unknowns in life that can easily keep us worrying. What if we could trust completely that God would take care of us and our loved ones. God is our rock and he alone will sustain us.

There will be many unknowns in your life. There will be moments when the rug feels as though it's been pulled out from under you and there is nothing to do but despair. In those moments that you can't control, you can trust. You can rest your soul, your mind, and your body in the hands of the one who has the power to sustain you.

What unknowns are you facing today? Can you rest in the knowledge that the Lord will sustain you?

Overcome the World

"I have told you these things, so that in me you may have peace.
In this world you will have trouble. But take heart!
I have overcome the world."

JOHN 16:33 NIV

There is no evil in this world that Christ has not already overcome.
He has accounted for everything that may happen to us and
guarantees that we can overcome it through his power. We can
take heart and have confidence knowing that we also have secured
victory because of the Lord Jesus' resurrection.

God has related his plan to us so we may have peace knowing that
our future with him is guaranteed. Regardless of what terrible
situations we face in this life, they will pass away. Christ's kingdom is
lasting and his victory is forever.

What trials shake your peace and cause you to doubt?
How has Christ demonstrated that he has also
overcome these trials?

Power without Limit

To him who is able to do immeasurably more than all we ask or imagine, according to his power that is at work within us, to him be glory in the church and in Christ Jesus throughout all generations, for ever and ever! Amen.

EPHESIANS 3:20-21 NIV

There is only so much that we can accomplish in our own strength. We plow through our tasks, and we can get a lot done. But we are limited in our power.

God has no limit in what he can do! If we ask him to work in our lives, there's no stopping the amazing things that will happen! We can accomplish more than we'd ever think to ask for. The best part is that he wants to do it for us. It's not a chore for him or another task to cross off his list so that you'll stop pestering him.

What bigger and bolder things can you ask God for today? Pray that he will give you the supernatural ability you need to accomplish all that's before you. His power is without limits, and he will extend it to you if you'll only ask him for it!

My Sheep

"I am the good shepherd.
The good shepherd lays down his life for the sheep."
JOHN 10:11 NIV

There is something soothing about the thought of sheep and shepherds, unless of course you are the one tending sheep. Herding, calling, feeding, leading, and gathering can't be all that easy. After all, aren't people a lot like sheep, and isn't life full of shepherding? Wouldn't it be nice at the end of a day to gather all our cares and leave them inside a pen to stay put for the night? Like scattered sheep, tasks leap through our minds. Shepherding is hard work.

Jesus picked up on the theme of sheep and shepherds. Shepherds in the Middle East often slept in the doorway of the sheepfold. The shepherd's body protected the sheep. With the shepherd as the gate, nobody could mess with the sheep. Jesus offered himself as the only way into the sheepfold. He is the only gate, and that knowledge provides comfort and peace. He gave us his Word to guide us and lead our steps. When the cares of our lives scatter through our nights like restless leaping sheep, God wants us to remember who blocks the doorway. No one guards and protects like he does. We can rest easy in his sheepfold.

What does Jesus as a good shepherd mean to you right now?

Hiding

Where can I go from your Spirit?
Where can I flee from your presence?
PSALM 139:7 NIV

These words were probably very similar to the ones Adam and Eve used in the garden when they were ashamed of their disobedience. It's how we feel when we are ashamed of something that we have done wrong. We want to hide and we don't want to be found!

It's okay to feel bad about doing the wrong thing and to feel guilty about making a wrong decision. But you can't live in that guilt and you can't hide forever. God already knows where you are. He is seeking restoration with you. His Spirit is already with you. If you are trying to run from him it's a losing battle! Instead, surrender to him and let his grace bring you joy.

Have you made poor choices lately? Do you know that this is the perfect time to run to God? He calls you out of hiding and removes your shame. Trust him to cover your mistakes and lead you in the better way.

Exaltation

"Be still, and know that I am God.
I will be exalted among the nations,
I will be exalted in the earth!"

PSALM 46:10 ESV

This psalm is not an invitation to be lazy, but to heed God. Children of God are expected to work hard, be responsible, and fulfill their duties. We are not, however, to frantically attempt to force our way through life ourselves, without heeding the Word of God or accepting his help and intervention.

When we rely on the power of our own strength, the temptation is to exalt ourselves. God is our source of strength, and he alone is to be exalted in the earth. He may choose at times to honor us as a good father does, but we should be glorifying him and recognizing his leadership in our lives.

*Do you take time to listen to God leading you
and correcting you?*

Approaching God

This is the confidence we have in approaching God:
that if we ask anything according to his will, he hears us.

1 JOHN 5:14 NIV

This verse should vanquish any idea Christians may have of God simply being a wishing well. Tossing prayers up to heaven and hoping for our own desires to be fulfilled is not how lovestruck, servant-hearted believers are expected to approach the Almighty.

When our deepest desire is for the Lord and for all people to come to know him, we pray to him for directions and answers that align with his agenda. That does not mean we have to vet our prayers or leave out details and requests that matter to us, but that everything comes under a covering of a mutual understanding that his master plan is what we are aiming at and hoping for above all else.

How can you learn what the will of God is,
so you can pray accordingly?

Whatever Comes

I will be strength to him
and I will give him my grace
to sustain him no matter what comes.

PSALM 89:21 TPT

This verse was God's promise to David when he chose him to be the king of Israel. We have the hindsight to know the mistakes and troubles that David went through. Scripture tells us David's story of blessing, sin, consequence, joy, battles, fear, and love.

David went through a lot in his life and the truth of this verse prevailed. God gave him grace and sustained him no matter what came. Let this verse be your promise today. Trust God to shower you with grace that will sustain you through everything you face today.

How can you face today with confidence
no matter what may come?

Life's Journey

He asked you for life, and you gave it to him—
length of days, for ever and ever.
Through the victories you gave, his glory is great;
you have bestowed on him splendor and majesty.
Surely you have granted him unending blessings
and made him glad with the joy of your presence.

PSALM 21:4-6 NIV

Though we commonly associate the words fear and fright with one another, they don't mean the same thing. Having a fear of the Lord means we respect him. It means we are in awe of him. He is, in fact, a God of great joy. When we seek to be fully in his presence, we can find that joy.

Our Father wants you to experience his joy. Unending blessings? Let's sign up for that! Shake off any old notions of dread or apprehension you may feel about being in his presence and seek the path of life he has set for you. He is a source of great delight. Rejoice in that knowledge today.

How can you respect God's goodness in your life?

Self-Control

Better to be patient than powerful;
better to have self-control than to conquer a city.
PROVERBS 16:32 NLT

What benefit is it to conquer a city if the other city had better intentions? If the Lord were to select someone to do a job, would it not make more sense that he chooses the one who is willing to listen to him and patiently wait for his instructions over the one who is more powerful?

Our power and our strength come from God as does our calling. Enacting skills he has given us brashly and arrogantly is unfitting for a child of God. He has equipped us in order to obey him. Therefore, having self-control and patiently waiting upon the Lord's instructions is of more worth than spoils from an entire city.

Have you asked the Lord how to use your skills and talents?

Rejoice

Be cheerful with joyous celebration in every season of life.
Let joy overflow, for you are united with the Anointed One!
PHILIPPIANS 4:4 TPT

True joy is so much more than mere happiness. As Christians, we rejoice because of the hope we have in Jesus. There will come a day when all our suffering and sorrows will be wiped away and we will finally be at home with our Lord. Understanding this powerful truth should fill us with a continual joy that is more real than our circumstances.

We should not overlook that when Paul penned these words, he was in jail for being wrongly accused. Just prior to his imprisonment, he had been shipwrecked, bitten by a snake, and placed under house arrest. Yet because of how aware he was of his eternal inheritance, nothing was able to steal his joy.

Do you think it is more difficult to choose to rejoice in horrible circumstances, or to remember to rejoice throughout the mundane activities of daily life? Why is joy always important?

Unfathomable

Do you not know? Have you not heard?
The LORD is the everlasting God,
the Creator of the ends of the earth.
He will not grow tired or weary,
and his understanding no one can fathom.

ISAIAH 40:28 NIV

Unlike us, the Lord never grows weary of doing good, not does he tire of loving us and acting lovingly toward us. He is the Creator of the universe, and he diligently upholds the world, governs it wisely, and judges it righteously. With vigor and strength, he provides for all his creation, from the birds to the grass to his beloved Church.

With an unfathomable understanding and infinite love that none of us could begin to grasp, he cares for all our needs out of his goodness. He understands each of us, considers our desires, and gives us all a unique calling. He is majestic and his ways are perfect. He has crafted everything with care and consideration. His eyes are always on us and he leads us in the path of righteouness. He is a good God who never grows weary.

*How is it different serving a God who understands
than one who is distant?*

Let Grace Win

If you bite and devour each other,
watch out or you will be destroyed by each other.
GALATIANS 5:15 NIV

Watching animals in the wild hunt, defend, and fight for territory can be brutal. We are not wild animals, but it might pay to stop and think about whether we are acting like them. When we start to assume or say unkind things about people, it can be the start of an attack on character or a judgement of the way things are being done.

God doesn't call us to be the judge of what others say or do, he wants us to have control of ourselves. Instead of being ready to attack or defend our territory, we should be quick to forgive, to try and understand others' perspectives, and stay out of the danger of judgement. Always let grace win. Let your heart be full of it so it spills over into the way you treat others.

Do you need to experience God's forgiveness for speaking unfairly about others? Do you need to receive healing for those who have hurt you?

A Pilgrimage

How blessed is the man whose strength is in You,
in whose heart are the highways to Zion!
PSALM 84:5 NASB

We are a go, go, go culture. We keep it running 24/7 as fast as we can. Do you have the courage to slow down? Too many of us are plagued by fear of missing out. This fear grips us to take life more at the speed of a motocross race and less the way it was intended to be: a pilgrimage. An exodus out of bondage and into freedom. Out of darkness, into light. Out of death, into resurrection. A pilgrimage is a slower journey, not a race run at remarkable speed.

We run quickly for two reasons: either we don't want to miss out, or we want to hurry up and get past all the hard stuff. You won't be rewarded for how fast you obtain the prize, or how much you accomplished along the way. On this exodus, quality matters. Miss out. Say no. Go slower. Don't give in to the temptation to run. Walk with Christ, allowing him to mature you as you move.

Are you going at a speed that is too fast?
Pray about what a slower pace could look like.

Not Destroyed

We are hard pressed on every side, but not crushed;
perplexed, but not in despair;
persecuted, but not abandoned;
struck down, but not destroyed.

2 CORINTHIANS 4:8-9 NIV

We are God's treasure in jars of clay. The Holy Spirit lives in us and enables us to have the power to accomplish all the Lord has called us to. This strength did not originate with us, but with the Spirit, and so our lives testify of God.

Just as jars of clay are, we may be battered and bruised in life. We may even shatter! But the treasure that is within is unbreakable. No matter what happens, we are not crushed, we do not despair, and we are never abandoned. What God has fashioned and redeemed cannot be destroyed.

Are you living as one who is indestructible?

No More Tears

You have delivered my soul from death,
my eyes from tears, my feet from stumbling.
PSALM 116:8 ESV

We are promised a time where there will be no more death, tears, or stumbling. This life is full of hardships, but we can live in hope that a day will come where joy will reign supreme. It is this hope that carries us through the hard times when we trust that God is still good and that he has good plans for us now and especially in the life to come.

Try to bravely face this day with joy concerning your future. This is not where it ends! Look forward to an eternity of joy, where the pain of this life will be no more. Thank God that even today he can bring relief to your physical pain, healing to your emotional pain, and restoration to your spiritual weakness. Lean on him through the hard times and he will give you strength to live with eternity in mind.

*How does the hope of a day with no more tears
help you through today?*

June

"The LORD is my strength and my defense;
he has become my salvation.
He is my God, and I will praise him,
my father's God, and I will exalt him."

EXODUS 15:2 NIV

Deep Contentment

I'm not telling you this because I'm in need,
for I have learned to be satisfied in any circumstance.
PHILIPPIANS 4:11 TPT

We can close our eyes and rest with ease when our worlds are in perfect harmony. It is easy to find peace in peaceful times. Happiness is at our fingertips and our steps are light and easy. In these seasons, it is effortless to raise our faces to the sky and say "Alleluia," and to declare his goodness. The struggle comes, though, when life isn't easy. When we are surrounded by heartbreak and disappointment. When grief feels suffocating, and hope seems so far away. When every day, even every moment seems impossible.

We forget in these times that true contentment, true joy, is still in our reach. We just have to open up our eyes and hearts to it. That seems easier said than done; however, when we learn to see joy in every circumstance, we are able to step bravely into each day set before us. Our circumstances do not define us; rather, joy becomes so rooted and engrained in who we are that finding peace becomes our second nature. True contentment, his genuine peace, cannot be easily shaken.

Is your contentment based on your present circumstances,
or is it rooted deeply in your faith in Christ?

Even Before That

Your eyes saw my unformed body;
all the days ordained for me were written in your book
before one of them came to be.

PSALM 139:16 NIV

We celebrate our birthdays as the day that our fully formed body came into the world and we breathed our first breath. Birthdays mark the beginning of our lives, but in this Scripture, God was celebrating you long before your birthday. He saw you before you were even formed; he knew that you were destined for life, even before that first breath. What an amazing God we have, who is not only all-knowing, but ever personal.

Take courage and strength from the truth that you were destined from the beginning and you have a wonderful purpose. Whatever you may be about to face in your day, hold your head high and remember the one who created you for such a time as this.

How can the knowledge of God's total attention on you change the way you step into your day?

Encouraging Bravery

When I am afraid, I will trust you.
I praise God for his word.
I trust God, so I am not afraid.
What can human beings do to me?

PSALM 56:3-4 NCV

We hear parents admonish their children not to be afraid. The older we get, the more there seems to be afraid of. Who can you encourage today, not by telling them to not be afraid, but by asking them to be brave? Asking people to mask their fear will only work temporarily at best. Asking them to make a choice for bravery gives them confidence in God's character and care.

Don't stuff down what you are feeling and move on by your own strength. Be brave in the situations that strike fear in you, knowing that God is fighting for you. Who do you know that needs to hear this today? Let God use you as his vessel to bring freedom. Help others remove their masks and hand them the bravery banner.

Who can you help to walk in bravery today?

O People

Trust in Him at all times, O people;
Pour out your heart before Him;
God is a refuge for us.
PSALM 62:8 NASB

We like to spend time on our personal relationship with God, and yet there is more to our faith than just ourselves. We were created to be in community with one another and one really important benefit of a close community is that we can be encouraged, or encourage others, in times of distress.

Think of the last time you felt really anxious or discouraged and reflect on who you were able to share those feelings with. Together we can pour out our hearts to him. We are all on this journey, not just individually, but walking alongside each other. Take a moment today to encourage the people you are walking with through life.

How can you be intentional about developing close relationships with those who encourage you in your faith and with those whom you need to encourage?

Spiritual Destination

Blessed are those whose strength is in you,
whose hearts are set on pilgrimage.
PSALM 84:5 NIV

We never really arrive at our spiritual destination of holiness and that's the way it is meant to be. The beauty is found where the heart is inclined toward finding the presence of God. This is our journey of faith in Christ. It is a pilgrimage in every sense of the word.

It might be a long and difficult terrain to navigate, but there will be wonders to see along the way and some profound insights and thoughts as you progress. This pilgrimage is one that ends at the most beautiful of places, one that your heart cannot fully comprehend. Enjoy the journey that you are on today.

*How can you appreciate the beauty of
your walk with God today?*

Uncomplicated Freedom

"I have swept away your offenses like a cloud,
your sins like the morning mist.
Return to me,
for I have redeemed you."

ISAIAH 44:22 NIV

We over-complicate freedom in the Christian life. Through our legalisms, we try to find a way to humanize the redeeming work of the cross because we simply can't wrap our minds around the supernatural character of God.

It can be hard to understand the complete grace offered at Calvary because we are incapable of giving that kind of grace. But when God says that he has forgotten our sin, and that he has made us new, he really means it. God is love, and love keeps no record of wrongs. Nothing can keep us from his love. Salvation tore the veil that separated us from the holiness of God. That complete work cannot be diminished or erased by anything we do.

Freedom is truly that simple. The beauty of the Gospel can be summed up in this single concept—grace, though undeserved, given without restraint. How can you accept this and walk in complete grace without question?

Powerful Virtues

Do you think lightly of the riches of His kindness and tolerance and patience, not knowing that the kindness of God leads you to repentance?
ROMANS 2:4 NASB

We tend to think of kindness, tolerance, and patience as some of the softer emotions. Consider however, the tolerance of a mother giving birth to a newborn, sacrificing her body and emotions for the love of a child. Think of the patience of a sister who sits alongside her sibling in the darkest days of her depression. Think of a daughter who cares diligently for her dying parent.

None of those actions are soft or meek. Kindness, tolerance, and patience can be fiercely, fervently, and powerfully loving. These Scriptures suggest that God's kindness, tolerance, and patience is exactly that—powerful enough to lead us to change our ways and never look back. This is nothing to think lightly of; it is life changing!

In what ways are the attributes of God
compelling you to change?

Beside Still Waters

He leads me beside still waters.
PSALM 23:2 ESV

We're all familiar with Psalm 23. The words are often featured on greeting cards and artwork. Have you wondered why God uses still waters in this chapter that he wrote to comfort us? Have you ever been by a quiet stream? The surface is so clear it's like a mirror. It reflects the peaceful beauty of God's creation. The water draws us to it and the silence and stillness invite us to also be motionless. Those still waters give us rest for our soul.

Can you think of anything that a stressed and grieving person could use more than calmness and restful silence? God knows what we need to restore our souls, to refresh us in our heartache. But it's hard to hear his words of comfort if we're zipping around. When we're still, we can hear God's soft whispers. We can draw close to the only one who can truly comfort an aching heart. After all, he grieved the loss of his beloved Son. Only someone who's walked the path of grief truly understands how we feel in our loss. And when God soothes our stress-filled soul, we won't lack for anything. He fills the empty places with his comfort as only he can.

Why do you think Psalm 23 is so popular?

Keeping a Secret

You can't trust a gossiper with a secret;
they'll just go blab it all.
Put your confidence instead in a trusted friend,
for he will be faithful to keep it in confidence.

PROVERBS 11:13 TPT

We've all been there before. A friend leans in and whispers, "Did you hear about what she did?" And something in us wants to be in the know. To hear the scoop. To spread the word. It's almost as if we are built to be mean girls. To share what we know of others' downfalls and fallacies.

It might feel good in the moment to tear people down because then we are not alone in the many ways we fall short. But it is a lie. We were designed to lift one another up. To be worthy of knowing a friend's secrets because we will keep the knowledge to ourselves. The next time you are tempted to share what isn't yours to tell, take a deep breath and pause. Ask yourself if betraying a confidence is worth letting down a friend. Instead, allow yourself to be the type of friend that the Lord has designed you to be.

How can you be a trusted friend?

Bless Someone

May he give you the desire of your heart
and make all your plans succeed.
PSALM 20:4 NIV

What a beautiful Scripture to read this morning. May God give you the desire of your heart and make your plans succeed. This is a great verse for you, but could it also be for someone else in your life? Think of someone in need of encouragement today and choose to pray this blessing over that person.

It might be your mother or father, someone you know has been unwell, perhaps it's the friend with a new baby, or someone who has just started a new job. Whatever that person's situation is, pray that God would make their plans succeed!

Did someone come to mind as you were reading this devotion?
How can you pray for them today?

His Strength

Look to the LORD and his strength;
seek his face always.

PSALM 105:4 NIV

Our natural instinct is to cry out to God in a panic and desperately search for him when we find ourselves in crisis. However, we don't have to panic or feel distressed in the face of the unknown. We can just ask him for help and he will be faithful to meet us. His strength is readily available. We can know the joy of his presence and the comfort and stability of his faithfulness.

God calms our racing and anxious thoughts with truth. He offers us wisdom and direction in the middle of decision making. He pierces the darkness that preys on us with his light. He fills us with gratitude and thanksgiving and renews our faith. He breathes bravery into our weak and timid souls.

*Do you draw strength from God both in times of need
and in times of peace?*

Hope

May the God of hope fill you with all joy and peace as you trust in him,
so that you may overflow with hope by the power of the Holy Spirit.

ROMANS 15:13 NIV

What differentiates hope from a wish? Think about the lottery. Does one hope to win, or wish to win? How about a promotion, a pregnancy, or a proposal? Both hoping and wishing contain desire, but for wishing, that is where it ends. Hope goes deeper. The strong desire for something good to happen is coupled with a reason to believe that it will.

We see then how vital hope is, and why it's such a beautiful gift. Desire without hope is empty, but together they bring joy, expectancy, and peace. When we put our hope in Christ, he becomes our reason to believe good things will happen. He is our hope.

How can you allow this blessing from Romans to wash over you today? Believe good things will happen—you have a wonderful reason to.

Righteous Answers

By awesome deeds you answer us with righteousness,
O God of our salvation,
the hope of all the ends of the earth
and of the farthest seas.

PSALM 65:5 ESV

What have you been asking of God lately? It could be healing from illness, prayer for someone close to you who is hurting, or maybe you just need a little help in your relationships. It is often said that God hears our prayers; yet you might feel like he has never answered yours.

God can seem very far away and unconcerned with your requests and needs. These feelings, however, are not the truth. The truth is that God is always very near to you. He knows your heart, he knows what you need, and he will answer. Trust him as you read this Scripture again and know that he will answer your prayers with amazing wonders and inspiring displays of power. Let this increase your faith today.

How can you allow God to be your hope that extends to the ends of the earth and farthest of seas?

A Place of Rest

The LORD is my shepherd; I shall not want.
He makes me lie down in green pastures.
PSALM 23:1 ESV

What is restful for you? Is there a place you like to go when you need to be refreshed? There's something special about enjoying the beauty of God's creation, and while we sit and take it in, we can almost feel the stress seeping away from us.

When we discover the beauty of creation—maybe a still lake, a canopy of leaves, a starry sky—a sweet peacefulness seeps into our souls. We find rest as we worship the one who is the author of beauty. Both our souls and bodies can be refreshed. Sometimes we don't have to get in our pajamas to find rest. We just need to look for Jesus. And when we find his fingerprints on the world he created, we need to make it a priority to spend time with him there, and discover rest for our souls.

Why is God's creation so restful? When's the last time you made it a priority to enjoy it? What can you do to make that happen more often?

The Desire Beneath

Since we know he hears us when we make our requests,
we also know that he will give us what we ask for.

1 JOHN 5:15 NLT

When birthdays or anniversaries are coming up, we often get asked about what we want as a gift. You may be someone that answers that easily, or you might take a while. Eventually you have an answer of what you would like or even need, but you never really know if you are going to get it, and you often have to wait until that significant day to find out!

We should be confident that God hears us when we tell him what we want or need. Perhaps we haven't had the confidence to voice it, but he knows our heart anyway. Could we consider that God knows the true desire behind our requests, and that this real desire is what we end up getting? It's a thought that might be worth pondering today.

What do you need or want from your heavenly Father?
Ask him, knowing he will hear you.

Praise through Circumstance

I have learned the secret of being content in any and every situation,
whether well fed or hungry, whether living in plenty or in want.
I can do all this through him who gives me strength.
PHILIPPIANS 4:12-13 NIV

When life is good, it is easy to praise God. My life is full of blessings, we think to ourselves. He is so good to me! But what happens when life is hard? Do we continue to give him the glory when we're thrown curveball after curveball?

Regardless of our circumstance, whatever our situation, we need to continue to give him the praises he so richly deserves. A life lived alongside Christ doesn't mean it will be one free of pain, of discomfort, of tough times. But it does mean that we can find contentment in it anyway because we have him in our lives to turn to. Pray for contentment today, whatever your circumstance. There is no crisis that the Lord is not willing to walk you through. You can do anything with him at your side!

How can you praise God today even if
circumstances aren't ideal?

Your Best Work

Whatever you do, work heartily, as for the Lord and not for men,
knowing that from the Lord you will receive the inheritance as your
reward. You are serving the Lord Christ.

COLOSSIANS 3:23-24 ESV

When our work is difficult, mundane, or thankless, we can
remember that everything we do is for the Lord. Out of appreciation
and love for him, we embrace every day's tasks with joy because
we serve the King! Even if our toils are for a difficult boss or
unappreciative children, our callings come from God and our
rewards do as well. We ought to put our best effort into our daily
grind, even if it seems to be devalued here on earth because it has
always been for God and not for mere man.

When others attempt to destroy your efforts, undermine your work,
or steal your success, continue you to serve with your whole heart
because that is what God has called you to act. The end results are in
his hands. You can trust him to bless your work. He is your reward.

How has the Lord called you to serve him today?

Crown of Joy

Those the LORD has rescued will return.
They will enter Zion with singing;
everlasting joy will crown their heads.
Gladness and joy will overtake them,
and sorrow and sighing will flee away.

ISAIAH 51:11 NIV

When the Lord rescued the Israelites out of Babylon and led them back to their own land, Jerusalem, there was great rejoicing and singing! Their sorrow was replaced by joy, for they had served in captivity for a long time. It was not the first time God had rescued them from slavery; Egypt was still fresh in their history. It also will not be the last time the Lord will rescue his people and lead them to their promised land.

When the Lord returns for his people again, we will finally enter his eternal promised land. Our sorrow and crying will be forever replaced with everlasting joy and singing. God never forgets his people. He has always made a way for his children to return to him when they go astray.

Why do you think the Psalmist refers to joy as a crown?

Strong

"Be strong and courageous and do the work. Don't be afraid or
discouraged, for the LORD God, my God, is with you.
He will not fail you or forsake you."

1 CHRONICLES 28:20 NLT

When the work before us is daunting, we may rush through it
or stall out in the process. Jesus has an answer for that. He says he
will not fail you or forsake you. To fail you would be to give you an
answer or technique that does not work for what you are supposed
to be doing. To forsake you would be to walk away from you in your
time of need.

If you truly believe God has done either of these to you, you really
need to sit in the quiet with your Bible and an open heart toward
God. He promises that if you seek him fully, you will find him. In
doing this, you will eradicate faulty thinking and get back on your
feet with the strength and courage to do what had once seemed
daunting. Jesus is with you!

*How can you apply today's principles
in an area where you hesitate?*

Surrender and Rest

"Come to me, all you who are weary and burdened, and I will give you rest. Take my yoke upon you and learn from me, for I am gentle and humble in heart, and you will find rest for your souls. For my yoke is easy and my burden is light."

MATTHEW 11:28-30 NIV

When we are faced with a problem our first instinct is to grab it and not let it go. We have this belief that if we hold onto it tightly, we have some sense of control. Often that sense is false. It creates anxiety and lets fear flourish. The more we struggle to hold on, the harder the situation becomes, and the more exhausting the fight.

The attitude that God wants us to have toward our problems is one of bravery. He asks us to choose surrender over having control. A huge part of that brave choice is having faith in him. By surrendering our fears and letting go of worry, we are trusting God. We can relax our grip, lift our eyes and hands to the sky, and breathe. No problem is too big or too difficult for God to handle. When we trust him, we can finally rest.

Do you trust God in every aspect of your life to surrender even those difficult parts to him?

Graciousness

Every time you give to the poor you make a loan to the Lord.
Don't worry—you'll be repaid in full for all the good you've done.
PROVERBS 19:17 TPT

When we give to those who cannot repay us, it is as if we are giving straight to God. The way we demonstrate our love for the Lord is by loving each other. When we are gracious to others, God will be gracious to us. When we forgive others, God will forgive us. When we give to others without an expectation for compensation, the Lord will certainly remember and repay us for our faithfulness.

The Lord is tremendously generous; we cannot outgive him. He sees every good deed and will not forget the generosity and grace we show to others. It is as if we are loving him directly. Our love for God can spur us on to love others. Rather than looking for what we can get, we should consider what we can give. God will reveal to us the needs in others that he wants us to meet. And we can serve without expecting anything in return because God sees and he will reward us.

Who can you give to, knowing they cannot return the favor?

The Good Lane

I would have despaired unless I had believed
that I would see the goodness of the LORD
In the land of the living.

PSALM 27:13 NASB

Do you ever catch yourself dwelling on the negative aspects of life? We can be nonchalant when someone tells us good news, but talk for hours about conflict, worries, and disappointment.

It is good to communicate things that aren't going so well in our lives, but we can also fall into the trap of setting our minds on the wrong things. Give your mind over to truth, honor, pure and lovely things today. You are sure to find goodness in unexpected places! Thank God for creating you with goodness in your heart.

How can you avoid the temptation of indulging in negative talk or harmful gossip today?

Time to Eat

They soon forgot what he had done
and did not wait for his plan to unfold.
PSALM 106:13 NIV

When you are asked about what you had for breakfast, can you even remember? With minds that are often full of so many things, forgetfulness can threaten to derail your appointments, friendships, and even your relationship with Jesus. It's not that Jesus will ever depart from you, but if you quickly forget the good and gracious things he has done, you are less likely to spend time communicating with him.

It is often in our moments of greatest joy that we forget about the source of that joy. Give yourself some space today to remember Jesus and what he has done in your life. Thank him for

all the times he has provided you with wisdom, peace, and assurance. Be grateful for the provision of a roof over your head and people around you that care for you.

How can you remember God's goodness today and every day?

Second Opinion

When you appear, I worship
while all of my enemies run in retreat.
They stumble and perish before your presence.

PSALM 9:3 TPT

When you go to the doctor about a condition that needs explaining, you might not always be confident in their diagnosis. People will usually encourage you to get a second opinion. There are times when significant people in your life have told you something about yourself that makes you feel terrible. They might have labelled you as selfish, or crazy, or any number of accusations.

This is your time to get a second opinion, so go straight to your heavenly Father and ask him what he thinks. This is your God, who created you and loves you unconditionally and sees nothing but the best, redeemed person that you are.

*Can you trust God to put your accusers to shame
when he shows up to cover you?*

Gems

Sweet friendships refresh the soul and awaken our hearts with joy,
for good friends are like the anointing oil
that yields the fragrant incense of God's presence.
PROVERBS 27:9 TPT

When you sign up for a competitive team sport, you have a basic understanding that you're going to have to work hard and that emotions will run high to win and succeed. You know that you'll win some, you'll lose some, and that somewhere along the way you'll start to feel good about playing the game whether you win or lose.

Playing a competitive team sport can sometimes feel the same as building relationships with other women. We win some—forming incredible relationships—and others we lose. We were created uniquely, and while we are asked to love one another, it doesn't mean that we hope for a best-friend relationship with each woman we meet.

Do you have a friend that holds you accountable but also lifts you up when you need it? Share how much that friend means to you today. If you're still looking for a close friend, don't lose heart. Pray for God to bring just the right person into your life.

Jesus Rep

Whatever you do, whether in word or deed,
do it all in the name of the Lord Jesus,
giving thanks to God the Father through him.
COLOSSIANS 3:17 NIV

When you work for a company or organization, you are expected to represent that particular brand or identity. Organizations who have a good reputation typically have a culture that their people are committed to being a part of. When you think of that company or brand, you can identify a certain value.

When you become a follower of Jesus, you also become his representative. Your personal relationship with Christ will inspire you to express something of his love, goodness, and grace to the world around you. You don't always need to shout that you are doing things in his name, you just need to simply be aware that your words and actions are influenced by his grace. Be encouraged today that you will represent him wherever you go.

What part of Christ do you know you are representing well,
and what might you need to let shine a little brighter
this week?

Confident in Incompetence

> It is not that we think we are qualified to do anything on our own.
> Our qualification comes from God.
>
> 2 CORINTHIANS 3:5 NLT

Whether bringing a brand new baby home from the hospital, giving your first major presentation at work, or simply making your first Thanksgiving meal, there's probably been at least one moment in your life that had you thinking, I have no idea what I'm doing. I'm not qualified. So what did you do? Chances are, you put a smile on your face, dove in, and did your best.

The older we get, the more we realize how truly helpless we are. We also, beautifully, realize it's okay. There is great freedom in admitting our shortcomings and allowing the Father to be our strength. No matter what he asks of us, we are confident in our incompetence. We may not be capable, but God is more than qualified to carry out his plans through us. All we need to do is swallow our pride and let him lead us.

What dream or calling would you be able to fulfill if you were to embrace God's competence as your own?

Secure Feeling

If you lie down, you will not be afraid;
when you lie down, your sleep will be sweet.
PROVERBS 3:24 ESV

Sweet sleep, that goal after a day filled with hectic schedules and cramped expectations, dissipates with the fast drumbeat of a fearful heart. We've all been there, eyes wide-open staring into a dark room, ears strained for sound, and our breath held. Insecurity pins us like a blanket wrapped too tight until bit by bit we feel ourselves relax again.

Proverbs talks about security resulting from God's wisdom. As we incorporate the Word of God into our lives, God brings a different kind of security. His security assures us as we end our day. He has walked with us during the hours past and will accompany us in the night ahead. Plan ahead to spend your last waking hours intentionally thinking through the blessings of your day. Look forward to thanksgiving as your head hits the pillow. Remember God's faithfulness throughout the day. Prepare for sweet sleep with confidence in God. Let truth relax your racing heart and taut muscles. When trust anchors to a secure God, frightening insecurities fade.

What makes you feel insecure?

Compassionate and Gracious

"The LORD, the LORD, the compassionate and gracious God,
slow to anger, abounding in love and faithfulness."
EXODUS 34:6 NIV

*E*ach day we walk with the Lord, we hope to mature in him. The more we learn about his character, his goodness and compassion, his mercy and his love, the more we yearn to be like him. It makes no difference whether you are a relatively new Christian or have been serving him for a long life. The more you know of God and his lovingkindness the more convinced you become to better yourself. To soften your heart. To be like him.

What more could we want in our heart of hearts than to be compassionate and gracious? Slow to anger? Abounding in love and faithfulness? Looking into our own character is not always enjoyable. We tend to be selfish and prideful. We may be ashamed of things we have said or done. God is faithful to forgive us for yesterday and before. We can take a courageous stand and declare each morning, "Today is a new day. Today I will be compassionate and gracious to those I meet. I will be slow to anger. I will abound in love. I will be more like Jesus."

*How did you show compassion this week? Can you identify a
time when you succeeded in slowing your anger?*

Worthy

You are worthy, our Lord and God, to receive glory and honor and power,
for you created all things, and by your will they were created
and have their being.

REVELATION 4:11 NIV

Within the vision God gave to John, he saw twenty-four elders before the throne of God. They were declaring the truths written in this verse. From God alone and for God alone do we exist and have a purpose. We are not an accident or an afterthought.

Creator God designed this world with all its wonder because it was his will. It is his will that we live, and he is therefore worthy of the praise of our lives. All glory, honor, and power are his, for we are nothing without him. Give him the honor he is due. Demonstrate the gratitude that you feel. God created you and gave you meaning. Uncover his purposes and declare his praises, for it is why you were made!

What do you think your main purpose in life is?

July

The LORD is a stronghold for the oppressed,
a stronghold in times of trouble.

PSALM 9:9 ESV

His Story

I will tell about the LORD's kindness and praise him for everything he has done. I will praise the LORD for the many good things he has given us and for his goodness to the people of Israel. He has shown great mercy to us and has been very kind to us.

ISAIAH 63:7 NCV

*Y*ou have a story to tell. When you think back over the years, reflect on the things that revealed God's goodness, graciousness, and love. Perhaps it was an illness or healing, a relationship or a relationship breakdown, it might have been a joy or a disappointment in your career. God is right next to us in all the things that life throws at us.

You may not have recognized him at the time, but hopefully you can attest to his kindness as you remember how you got through those times. This is your story and just like the Israelites, it is worth telling and repeating. Your story is important, so be brave and speak it out!

Where can you see God's goodness, mercy, or kindness in your present circumstance?

Grace upon Grace

For of His fullness we have all received,
and grace upon grace.
JOHN 1:16 NASB

*Y*ou know those days, the perfect ones? Your hair looks great, you nail a work assignment (whether client presentation, spreadsheet, or getting twins to nap at the same time), you say just the right thing and make someone's day, and then come home to find dinner waiting for you. It's good upon good, blessing upon blessing.

Being a daughter of the Almighty gains us access to that blessed feeling every day, even when our circumstances are ordinary or even difficult. His love is so full, and his grace so boundless, that when his Spirit lives in us even a flat tire can feel like a blessing. Our status as beloved daughters of the King guarantees it, we need only claim it.

Do you see God's grace poured out upon you today?
Thank him for it.

Rebuilding

The LORD will rebuild Jerusalem;
there his glory will be seen.
PSALM 102:16 NCV

You will have a lot of thoughts about your day ahead—grocery lists, medical appointments, sports training, or where you put those keys! We are so consumed with our thoughts of all of the details of the day ahead that we forget to think on the greatness of God.

When we allow our thoughts of God to take over, we see our small concerns about the day fall away. Ask God to break through your stresses and help you concentrate on what matters the most today. Thank him that in the times of deepest need he is the water of life you can draw your strength from.

How can you drink of God's living water today?

Changing Seasons

He made the moon to mark the seasons;
the sun knows its time for setting.
PSALM 104:19 ESV

You will, undoubtedly, have various seasons in your life: seasons of longing and contentment, seasons of discouragement and joy, seasons of more and less. Being a grown-up means stretching into new ways of living, and this usually doesn't happen until the season hits.

Don't make excuses for why you can't do what God is calling you to do. Be brave! God will not move you into something without giving you the grace you need to make it through. The Lord has placed a calling on your life, and he will give you the courage to know that he is with you when he calls you to step forward.

What season are you in right now?
Do you feel God calling you into something new?

Things Unknown

"Thus says the LORD who made it, the LORD who formed it to establish it (the LORD is His name): 'Call to Me, and I will answer you, and show you great and mighty things, which you do not know.'"

JEREMIAH 33:2-3 NKJV

"If you're there God, give me a sign!" People have screamed this into the heavens many times throughout the years. We want to see something that will tell us that God is real—and not just real, but also present. We want that experience that will bring heaven to earth and expel our doubt with a single lightning bolt. God is more than able to give us those miraculous signs as we have seen countless times throughout the Bible and throughout history. But he is so much more than experience.

We mistakenly think experience is the peak of his power. Other gods can perform miracles and deliver experiences, but the one true God continues to show his power in the valley. He is even in the valley of the shadow of death where miracles seem non-existent. Those other gods have nothing to offer us in despair. God will show us great and mighty things. He is not limited by time, space, or human understanding. Put your hope and faith in the God who is.

What signs are you looking for from God right now?

Words Matter

Do not let any unwholesome talk come out of your mouths,
but only what is helpful for building others up according to their needs,
that it may benefit those who listen.
 EPHESIANS 4:29 NIV

Whoever told us words can't hurt us was clearly mistaken. Their intentions may have been good, but the reality is that words do hurt. Words do matter. Taunts, rants, and criticisms hurt the hearers, and God has called us to build up one another. Old habits die hard, but you can break those habits. How you speak with others will define you. Do your friends consider you trustworthy or incapable of keeping a secret? Do you use your words as a weapon, or are your conversations encouraging and helpful?

We are reminded in Scripture that keeping our conversations wholesome and heartwarming can be gratifying and cheering for both speakers and hearers. Choose your words and conversations carefully. Take a moment to gather your thoughts before speaking and especially before responding to someone else. Don't return one mean statement with another. Being kind in thought, word, and deed are qualities to aim for.

Can you think of one or two changes you would like to make in the way you speak to others?

Listening to God

After the earthquake came a fire,
but the Lord was not in the fire.
And after the fire came a gentle whisper.

1 KINGS 19:12 NIV

A surprising study on parenting styles revealed that one of the best ways to get the attention of a child is to whisper. When instructing an important lesson, imparting it in a whisper helps the child to focus, to remember, and to act upon the information. Yelling or pontificating doesn't work as well. Taking the child onto your lap or sitting closely and softly speaking causes both memory and comprehension to improve. This is true with your heavenly Father. He wants to share so very much with you. He wants to gather you up in his arms and give you strength.

God longs to tell you of his unfathomable love for you. He wants to lighten your burdens and help you grow. Are you willing to listen to his still, small voice? Let him whisper in your ear. Our lives are noisy, and we need to slow down, be quiet, and listen to God. Take a deep breath, sink back into his arms, and allow God to feed your soul.

Have you listened quietly to God? Have you heard him?
What do you think God wants to tell you?

Confident Trust

Do not throw away this confident trust in the Lord.
Remember the great reward it brings you!
HEBREWS 10:35 NLT

After an entire book dedicated to validating and strengthening a Christian's confidence in Christ, this warning is issued: do not lose it. Maintain your confidence and trust in God. In the end, it will be rewarded.

The best way to remain confident is by remembering the truths of the Gospel. We must immerse ourselves regularly in the Word so the subtle lies and twisting of truth that the world constantly bombards us with do not begin to corrupt our confidence. Hold fast to the Father and ask for wisdom to discern truth from the lies. Confidently stand on faith in him alone. He is the only way.

Do you surround yourself with truth?
What sort of messages are you being told daily?

Power

"You will receive power
when the Holy Spirit comes on you."
ACTS 1:8 NIV

After Jesus's ascension, he gave the promised gift of the Holy Spirit to the disciples. They were told to wait for this gift before they proceeded any further. Jesus knew it would be fruitless to attempt to carry out any exploits unless his followers were filled with his Spirit. As they waited, the Holy Spirit came and filled them with power. This was a power they lacked prior to this moment. It wasn't something they could conjure up on their own. Jesus wanted them to know that a new power would come.

That same power is there for all of us who ask. God hasn't given us a spirit of fear but one of power. You don't need your own power, God will give you his through the Holy Spirit.

*Have you asked the Lord for his power through the Holy Spirit
or do you lean on your own strength?*

Assembling Together

*Let us consider how to stimulate one another to love and good deeds,
not forsaking our own assembling together, as is the habit of some.*
HEBREWS 10:24 NASB

All throughout Scripture, God's intention for us to live as a community of believers is revealed. He created us to need each other so we could learn how to put others first and lay ourselves down. Here, we are reminded to encourage others toward love and good works.

We have a biblical responsibility to fellowship with others so that we can continue to learn and grow through relationships, and so we can help bear their burdens and encourage them. Relationships can be the most difficult element in life to navigate. Rather than moving on when they become strained or require maintenance, fight for love and unity with God's strength.

*When it becomes difficult to be around someone,
how do you respond to the situation? Do you humble yourself
and attempt to amend the relationship?*

Gift of Rest

*Let us think of ways to motivate one another
to acts of love and good works.*
HEBREWS 10:24 NLT

Amusement appeared on faces throughout the restaurant as the group approached the hostess stand. This wasn't your normal group of friends out for a fun and restful night. No, it's not every day you see five dads out for the evening with their fifteen collective children. Fifteen! Babies in arms. Toddlers clutching their daddy's hand. And an assortment of boys and girls ranging from about three to twelve. Daddy's Day Care had arrived complete with wiggles and giggles. But they made it through the evening of controlled chaos and arrived home with all their children. Those dads were there with all the kids because they had given their wives a weekend to rest.

Rest is a gift we can give to others who desperately need it. Ask God to show you a single parent, an elderly person, a caregiver, or a weary mom who needs some rest, and then become God's hands and feet to provide those moments for them. Give someone the gift of rest and discover the blessing during the process.

*Think of two people who need rest. What are some specific
steps you can take to help them?*

Strength

Be strong in the Lord
and in his mighty power.
EPHESIANS 6:10 NLT

*P*aul did not undercut the importance of the spiritual battles we engage with. He wrote often about how we are in a war against evil and cautioned us to be alert to it. Just prior to describing a detailed metaphor of suiting up in spiritual armor with each of its specific components, he gave the most necessary piece of battleplan advice: "Be strong in the Lord."

God is ready and willing to give us everything we need for any situation. Often, however, he will wait for us to ask so we are reminded that he is our source of strength and that we should always be turned toward him.

What other battleplans does the book of Ephesians offer?

Natural Response

Bear with each other, and forgive each other.
If someone does wrong to you,
forgive that person because the Lord forgave you.
COLOSSIANS 3:13 NCV

As family members, we should be quick to forgive and to help each other succeed. If we truly understand what Christ did for us and what he saved us from, then forgiveness should be our natural response. Everything we have is because of the grace of God poured on us, so we are to show each other the same grace.

This verse is not instructing us to be apathetic toward sin or stay silent in the face of injustice but to forgive the wrongs done to us and help others to bear the burdens of their weaknesses. This way, growth can occur and the grace we have been shown is made evident by the way we show grace to others.

Is there anyone you need to forgive today?

Victory in Christ

The God of peace will soon crush Satan under your feet.
The grace of our Lord Jesus be with you.
ROMANS 16:20 NIV

As we continue to follow the ways of truth and godliness, the enemy also persists in his attempts to thwart us. Paul warned the people of false teachers and doctrine, which is one of the devil's crafty ways of undermining the work of Christ and Christians. God gives us the promise, however, that these attacks will ultimately fail and our enemy will be struck down! Everything that is a lie will fall away and only what is true will remain.

Through all of life's trials and the deception of others, we are given the promise that Jesus' grace will be with us. All the calamity and lies of the world cannot derail us from following Christ when we have been given the gifts of grace, peace, and truth.

How do Paul's words associate with God's prophetic promise in Genesis 3:15?

Labor in the Lord

My dear brothers and sisters, stand firm. Let nothing move you.
Always give yourselves fully to the work of the Lord,
because you know that your labor in the Lord is not in vain.

1 CORINTHIANS 15:58 NIV

At the conclusion of his letter, Paul offers his dear Corinthian brothers and sisters a final exhortation. First, they should stand firm, be steadfast, be faithful, and keep going. Continue in the teaching of the Lord and don't grow weary or be sidetracked. Second, Paul says to be immovable. Do not compromise values or conform to the culture out of pressure. Stand on the Word of God and do not be tossed around by a light form of Christianity.

Finally, Christians are to give themselves fully to their calling. Embrace the work the Lord calls us to and understand that it holds eternal importance. The fruit of our labor will not fade away because we serve an eternal Lord who remembers every act of faith.

What work has God given you to do?
How can you give yourself fully to it?

Hidden Beauty

Let your adorning be the hidden person of the heart with the imperishable beauty of a gentle and quiet spirit, which in God's sight is very precious.

1 PETER 3:4 ESV

Beauty is a powerful influencer in the lives of women. We are constantly bombarded with images and messages of what beauty is and what it should be. Even if we are confident in who we are, it can still be difficult not to give in to the subtle thoughts of not being good enough. The awful truth about outward beauty is that no matter how much time, attention, and investment you put into it, beauty can never really last. Our appearance inevitably changes over time, and our physical beauty does fade.

In a world where we are constantly told to beautify ourselves so we will be noticed, the concept of adorning the hidden person of the heart sounds almost make-believe. But what it comes down to is the truth that the most important opinion we should seek is the opinion of our Creator. It might sound trite or cliché, but when we step away from the distraction of the media circus and all the lies it's told us, the truth becomes clear.

Did you know that you were made to delight the heart of God?

One Voice

May the God of endurance and encouragement grant you to live in such harmony with one another, in accord with Christ Jesus, that together you may with one voice glorify the God and Father of our Lord Jesus Christ.

ROMANS 15:5-6 ESV

By God's grace, we press on. This life is wrought with difficulties and our own perseverance will at some point expire. God's grace has no end. He will always offer us the endurance and encouragement we need.

Often, God's mode of communication is through other believers. This is one more reason why it is so vital that we live harmoniously together, pursuing peace and having grace. Just like when we're singing a song with others, we each have our own part but we blend voices to sing together with one united voice.

Why does God want you to learn to sing with others instead of just performing a solo?

Chalkboard

The humble will see their God at work and be glad.
Let all who seek God's help be encouraged.

PSALM 69:32 NLT

Chalkboards are almost extinct these days, but if you've ever tried to write on a wet one, you'll know that the writing doesn't show up well—until the board and the chalk dry. It's an interesting process to watch the letters and words that were once faded become clear and strong. Colors become sharper and bolder.

This is how our faith can be at times. It sometimes feels like it has been wiped clear and we feel hazy just like that wet chalkboard. But God has begun to write and draw in this space. Have patience in these times because what is about to appear is beautiful, clear, and bold. God is doing something even though you can't quite make it out yet.

How do you see God at work in your life today?

Old Age

The righteous will flourish like a palm tree.
They will still bear fruit in old age.

PSALM 92:12, 14 NIV

*C*hildren of God are often compared with trees in Scripture. Trees have a root system, branches, and often bear fruit. In addition, trees don't necessarily weaken with age. In fact, many trees become stronger as they age.

While our human body ages, there comes a point when it is no longer growing stronger. However, that is only our flesh. Our inner man can actually grow in strength even though our frame does not. As we are growing in strength in God, we are still able to bear much fruit later into life. Good, tasty, ripe fruit doesn't come to the young, baby Christians. It comes to those seasoned wise souls whose roots are as thick and strong as their branches.

Have you bought into the mindset of our culture that dreads aging? Are you trying to avoid aging? Will you accomplish anything by attempting this?

Greater Joy

You have given me greater joy
than those who have abundant harvests
of grain and new wine.
PSALM 4:7 NLT

Comparison is something that we face daily. We are confronted every morning with people who have more or less than we do. We see cars on the road that are nicer than ours, people with great fashion sense, and those creative people who seem to make everything look nice.

Social media is filled with pictures of vacations, celebrations, and great achievements. It's important in these times to anchor your self-worth in the joy that you have in Jesus. Get some perspective when you feel like everyone else is doing life better than you! Be happy for them but overflow with joy for yourself because you are an heir of the King!

How can you face the many comparisons that creep in through social media? How do you continue to be fully grounded in God's eternal love?

Neverending Joy

My heart rejoices in the LORD!
The Lord has made me strong.
Now I have an answer for my enemies;
I rejoice because you rescued me.
No one is holy like the LORD!
There is no one besides you;
there is no Rock like our God.

1 SAMUEL 2:1, 2 NLT

Consider for a moment the most joyous time of your walk with Christ. Imagine the delight of that season, the lightness and pleasure in your heart. Rest in the memory for a minute, and let the emotions come back to you. Is the joy returning? Do you feel it? Now, hear this truth: The way you felt about God at the highest, most joyful, amazing, glorious moment is how he feels about you at all times.

What a glorious blessing! Our joy is an overflow of his heart's joy toward us; it is just one of the many blessings God showers over us. The season of your greatest rejoicing can be now, when you consider the strength he provides, the suffering from which you have been rescued, and the rock that is our God. His blessings don't depend on our feeling joyous; we experience joy because we realize God's gracious and loving blessings.

How can you lift your praises to God today?

More Compassion

The LORD is compassionate and gracious,
Slow to anger and abounding in lovingkindness.
PSALM 103:8 NASB

Consider the Israelites wandering in the desert: God had rescued them out of bondage and went before them in a pillar of fire, providing for their every need and protecting them. What did they offer back to him? Complaints.

God loves his children regardless of their sin, their past, and their failings. We aren't dealt with as we deserve; rather, according to his great love for us. Can we say the same about how we treat those around us? Are we compassionate, slow to anger, and full of love? Or are we offended, impatient, and aggravated?

How can you be slow to anger and show compassion that is beyond human capability?

A Day at the Spa

Pour out all your worries and stress upon him and leave them there,
for he always tenderly cares for you.

1 PETER 5:7 TPT

Could you use a day at the spa? A day of indulgence guarantees a soothing atmosphere and rest and relaxation for stressed bodies and minds. Unfortunately, many of us don't make time for ourselves like we should, and money is sometimes difficult to scrape together for extras.

Did you know that there's an even better spa? God's spa for the soul. Make time to hang out there. The good news is that it's free. God begins by clothing us with righteousness and then detoxes our hearts to remove impurities. He gives us special times to be still and hang out with him, refreshing us as nothing else can do. Are you stressed? Choose the treatment of God's Word. Soak in the sweet promises that you'll find there. Massage away your cares with time in prayer. The aches and pains of your soul will disappear. When you fill your heart with Jesus, your mind will be at rest. And you'll discover there's always an appointment available for you.

What do you most need from God's spa for the soul? How does spending time with him invigorate and refresh you?

Take the Plunge

You will show me the way of life,
granting me the joy of your presence
and the pleasures of living with you forever.

PSALM 16:11 NLT

*D*aredevil divers plunge from cliffs one-hundred-thirty-five feet high into the gurgling warm seas of the Pacific Ocean in Acapulco, Mexico. It's like a giant bubble bath when they land in the frothy warm water, but what a scary leap before that. Can you imagine the rapid heartbeat of these divers just before taking that daring jump? God promises to be with us during our challenging and stressful times, but he'll also accompany us on those exhilarating and fun adventures too. After all, God is the creator of everything. That means he made those exciting adventures.

Sometimes we're guilty of thinking of God as a problem-solver—which he is—but maybe we haven't ever viewed him as the life of the party. God gives life and he promises it abundantly. Our walk with him should be an adventure every single day—one where stress and anxiety disappear. The greatest adventure of all times is walking with Jesus. It doesn't get any more exciting than the joy of his presence and the pleasure of eternal life with him.

How can a new adventure take away the stress of a long day?

Loving Shepherd

When he saw the crowds, he had compassion on them,
because they were harassed and helpless,
like sheep without a shepherd.
MATTHEW 9:36 NIV

*D*eep down inside of each of us is a desire to not only be seen,
but to also be taken care of. When we feel broken down and bruised,
there is nothing more inviting than a loving hand. Someone
who sees our hurts and mends each one. The world is cold and
sometimes heartless. There are times in life where we feel exhausted
and unseen. We are desperate for someone to love us in the ways we
were created to be loved.

We can depend on God to take care of every single need. He takes
great care and delight in wiping our tears, speaking life and truth
back into our souls, and calming the storms that rage within. He is
our resting place. He is faithful to meet every one of our needs with
his goodness. He does not leave us wanting, rather he fills us up, so
we are overflowing with his peace and love. He did not create in us a
need to be loved, to be left unloved. He loves each of us like no other
ever can.

*Do you feel weary and tired? Let the Lord carry you
to still waters, and rest in him.*

Meditate on Goodness

Whatever is true, whatever is honorable, whatever is right, whatever is pure, whatever is lovely, whatever is of good repute, if there is any excellence and if anything worthy of praise, dwell on these things.

PHILIPPIANS 4:8 NASB

Do you ever catch yourself dwelling on the negative aspects of life? We can be nonchalant when someone tells us good news, but talk for hours about conflict, worries, and disappointment. It is good to communicate things that aren't going so well in our lives, but we can also fall into the trap of setting our minds on the wrong things.

Paul saw the need to address this within the church of Philippi. It seems there were people in the church that thought too highly of themselves and allowed discord to reside in their midst. Think of what dwelling on the negative actually does: it creates feelings of hopelessness, discouragement, and a lack of trust in our God who is good, true, and just.

Do you need to ask for forgiveness for a heart that has been too negative? Can you find anything in your life and the lives of others that have virtue or are worthy of praise?

The Burning Bush

"When forty years had passed, an Angel of the Lord appeared to him in a flame of fire in a bush, in the wilderness of Mount Sinai."
ACTS 7:30 NKJV

*D*o you ever feel like your life is in a holding pattern? Like your something big must be lurking around the next corner. You may feel like your life is being wasted while you wait for your own destiny.

God had Moses in a very similar holding pattern. He had this incredible experience at birth where he was specifically saved from certain death, miraculously found by the most powerful woman in the land, and raised as royalty. He had an unbelievable launch to his life, and then, after a fatal mistake, he became your average sheep herder in the desert for the next forty years. Forty years. That's a long time to wonder if the greatness of the vision you were born into will ever come to fruition.

If you feel directionless right now—without vision and without destiny—know that no wilderness is too remote for you to stumble upon a burning bush. Can you trust, watch, and wait?

Struggling to Pray

He is able also to save forever those who draw near to God through Him,
since He always lives to make intercession for them.

HEBREWS 7:25 NASB

*D*o you ever sit down to pray and find yourself struggling to find
the words to begin? You stumble over your words, your mind draws
a blank. You want to be obedient by spending time with the Lord,
but you don't even know where to begin.

The good news is that God intervenes for us in the midst of every
type of struggle, including our prayer life. He's got our back in times
of pain and misery. Why wouldn't he be there for us when we want
to converse with him? He will give us the words to say when we find
ourselves lacking. In fact, he will even go beyond that and give you a
form of communication that words can't express!

*When you find yourself searching for the right way to express
what you want to say to God, do you know that he will
intercede if you allow him to? Spend some time sitting quietly,
and let him takes the reins for you today. He knows your heart!*

Building It Up

> "Every kingdom divided against itself will be ruined,
> and every city or household divided against itself will not stand."
> MATTHEW 12:25 NIV

Do you remember a moment when you realized you just couldn't do it on your own? Today's culture encourages us to be independent. We can drive where we want, choose our own education, and decide what communities to belong to. This freedom of choice is a gift, and yet it can also lead to us feeling as though we are the masters of our own destiny. As independent as the modern life may be, we are still part of many social structures.

This means that at some point, you will need to rely on others. It's better to learn how to live in harmony with others than to see your workplace, church, or home become divided. If you are in a situation now where you are starting to see division, don't become part of the problem. Taking sides will only cause more fractures. We are called to unity, because this is what makes us all stronger and better people.

What kingdoms, cities and households are you part of? How can you work toward building up these things?

Perseverance

Do not throw away this confident trust in the Lord. Remember the
great reward it brings you! Patient endurance is what you need now,
so that you will continue to do God's will. Then you will receive
all that he has promised.

HEBREWS 10:35-36 NLT

Do you remember when you first decided to follow Christ?
Maybe you felt like a huge weight was being lifted off you, or that the
peace and joy you'd been searching for was finally yours. You were
filled with excitement in your newfound life, and you felt ready to
take on the world in the name of Jesus.

Following God may come easy at first. We accept him into our lives
and are swept into his love with incredible hope. But as time goes
on, old temptations return, and threaten to shake our resolve. The
confidence we felt in our relationship at first lessens as we wonder if
we have what it takes to stick it out in this Christian life.

*Perhaps you have lost the confidence you had at first. Or
maybe you are still in that place of complete confidence and
trust. Either way, can you step boldly forward into all that God
has for you? Remain confident in him; he will accomplish
what he has promised.*

Limitless

Continually they turned back from him
and wounded the Holy One!
They forgot his great love, how he took them by his hand
and with redemption's kiss he delivered them from their enemies.

PSALM 78:41-42 TPT

Do you struggle with where you fit? Are you on a hunt to find your purpose? Do you feel like you've changed, and the purpose you thought God had for you seems vastly different now? It can be so confusing, can't it? When we think our purpose is unclear, we can easily become blind to God's capacity.

Friends, God has no capacity. We serve a God without limits. He tells us that, in him, anything is possible. You don't need to have confidence in what you can do—only in what he can accomplish through you. He is capable of absolutely anything, and his plans for you run deep.

What do you feel your purpose is? Open your heart and mind to a limitless God. Believe, deep in your heart, the fullness of his limitless capability for you. Pray on that, take steps, and watch him fulfill your meaningful purpose.

August

You will keep in perfect peace
those whose minds are steadfast,
because they trust in you.

ISAIAH 26:3 NIV

Every Talent Counts

The LORD has given them special skills as engravers, designers, embroiderers in blue, purple, and scarlet thread on fine linen cloth, and weavers. They excel as craftsmen and as designers, embroiderers in blue, purple, and scarlet thread on fine linen cloth, and weavers. They excel as craftsmen and as designers.

EXODUS 35:35 NLT

During World War I, the American Red Cross called on American citizens to assist the troops fighting overseas. One of their greatest successes was a knitting campaign called Knit Your Bit, which required only knitting needles, wool, and an easily-learned skill. At the end of the war, Americans had produced 24 million military garments, including sweaters, helmet-liners, and socks. Men, women, boys, and girls all contributed to the effort. No skill was too little, no contribution too insignificant, to answer the call.

In the same way, your creative skills are a gift to the kingdom of God. Your imagination can be used for his glory! You may think God isn't interested in using your creativity. But your gifts are a great blessing to others. Where might your efforts be a blessing? Do you know someone who could benefit from your thoughtfulness? Your humble offerings bear witness of God's love!

Prayerfully consider how to use your gifts for his purposes?

Bold and Confident

My voice You shall hear in the morning, O LORD;
In the morning I will direct it to You,
And I will look up.

PSALM 5:3 NKJV

Each and every day, we are given the most incredible opportunity. We are given the chance to talk to a God who has been in our shoes. A man who literally walked the walk. He is waiting for us to walk up to him and ask him anything.

Jesus went through the same things we do during his time on earth, so he truly understands where we're coming from when we approach him. We don't need to muster up our courage! He wants us to be confident. Esther was bold when she approached her king about saving her people, and that guy was known to make rash and terrible decisions! We get to talk to a King who is known for his mercy.

Are you holding back tentatively in your time with your heavenly King? Be bold, and be confident! He will show you grace and mercy in whatever it is that you seek.

Builders of Humans

> Encourage the hearts of your fellow believers and support one another,
> just as you have already been doing.
>
> 1 THESSALONIANS 5:11 TPT

*E*ach of us is a builder when we walk through growth with another believer. We are a house for God as well as for ourselves. We are a temple and one of the Holy Spirit's places of habitation. When we are encouraged, we take on greater faith that God is constructing us according to his will. When we invest time and energy into learning from others we grow and create a better house in which the Holy Spirit dwells.

All we do is for the glory of God. When we encourage others, and share our testimonies, insights, and lessons learned, we become construction workers who build humans. What a wonderful joy it is to create a glorious habitation for Christ's Spirit. What a wonderful honor it is to help others do the same.

When you consider your inner life, what do you want to offer to Christ for an upgrade? Be bold.

Fully Alive

When you follow the revelation of the Word,
heaven's bliss fills your soul.
PROVERBS 29:18 TPT

*E*veryday living can suck the life right out of us. Somewhere in the middle of being stuck in traffic, sweeping floors, and brushing our teeth, we can forget to be alive. What does it mean to be alive, rather than just to live? Not to only exist in life, but to know it, to understand it, to experience it—to live it. What would it be like? Freefalling from an airplane. Running through the grass barefoot with sun on your face. Bringing babies into the world, screaming and strong with power and life.

What would it be like if we lived each moment in the spirit of those fully alive moments? Without a reason for life, without purpose, we perish. We falter. We lose our way. We lose hope. We begin to casually exist instead of breathing in the reverence of a fully alive life. We need to re-cast vision for ourselves daily. Open your mind and your heart to the vision that God has for you.

Are there dreams God has given you that you've lost along the way? Trust that they will be returned to you. God breathed life into you so you could live it to the fullest.

Embracing Solitude

After sending them home, he went up into the hills by himself to pray.
Night fell while he was there alone.
MATTHEW 14:23 NLT

*E*veryone in the house is gone—for the entire weekend. How did those words make you feel? Were you considering who to call for a fun night out, or reveling in the thought of hours of uninterrupted quiet time to read, relax, and restore? Perhaps both ideas appeal to you: a little girl time, and a little alone time.

Jesus cherished his alone time. He guarded it. Amidst the stories of ministering to crowds, feeding thousands, and untold hours spent with the twelve he chose as apostles, it's easy to miss this fact. Studying the gospels, we see a pattern emerge: he healed, then he went off to pray alone; he taught, then he climbed the mountain to pray alone; the disciples went out on the boat, and Jesus remained on the shore—alone.

Imagine Jesus slipping off, unnoticed, and going to spend time with his Father. What intimacy they must have shared; how restorative those hours of prayer must have been. Whatever your feelings about solitude, can you ask God to give you his heart for alone time with you?

Being Still

The LORD will fight for you;
you need only to be still.
EXODUS 14:14 NIV

For some of us, being still, is very difficult, especially when we are facing crisis or uncertainty. We prefer to be in control, doing, moving. Our fears take over and propel us to keep going. In many ways we gain a sense of security by having a plan and seeing that plan carried out perfectly. But sometimes our refusal to pause is a reflection of our lack of faith. God wants us to be still, to surrender, to let go, and let him.

In our stillness we are able to hear God's voice and see him working clearly. We can release the tight grasp we have of our plans and surrender them to the one who has our best interests at heart. In our stillness he can quiet our anxieties and worries. In him we can be still when the world is crumbling, when uncertainty is present, and in our pain and hurt.

Do you struggle to slow down and be still? Is your inability to surrender control a reflection of your lack of trust in God?

Joy of the Righteous

May the righteous be glad and rejoice before God;
may they be happy and joyful.

PSALM 68:3 NIV

God did not come from us; we came from God. Our sole purpose is intermingled with our service to him. He has given each of us a calling, and it is our delight to learn to walk the path he has put us on. So then, unlike others who may scramble for fleeting happiness, we have true joy in doing the work of the Lord.

We rejoice in God because he satisfies our souls. Our longing and our loneliness fade away and are replaced with joy and contentment. As God's righteous people, it is our both our mandate and our gladness to follow the Lord's commands.

Does obedience still give you joy
even if you do not want to obey?

Suffering

I'm not defeated by my weakness, but delighted! For when I feel my weakness and endure mistreatment—when I'm surrounded with troubles on every side and face persecution because of my love for Christ—I am made yet stronger. For my weakness becomes a portal to God's power.

2 CORINTHIANS 12:10 TPT

God does not delight in your suffering. Many may read through the Bible and think God takes pleasure in our suffering. Nothing could be further from the truth. What God does want to accomplish in your life is holiness. Often it takes insults, hardships, persecutions, and troubles to humble us before God. Our best life is not one free of suffering, but one totally reliant on God's grace.

If you look back a couple of verses, it speaks of how Paul was being harassed. This was directly from Satan—and what Satan intended to harm and discourage him with was used to bring Paul to his knees before God in humility. If whatever is thrown our way is constantly keeping us from becoming puffed up with self-reliant pride and on our knees before God, let it come! God is not delighting in your pain. Though relief may not come, God is at work in you through it.

How does this passage change your view of suffering?

The Good Fight

I remind you to fan into flame the gift of God, which is in you…for the
Spirit God gave us does not make us timid, but gives us power,
love and self-discipline…join with me in suffering for the gospel,
by the power of God.

2 TIMOTHY 1:6-8 NIV

God has asked us to join him in the fight for his kingdom.
In order to feel confident in what that looks like, we need to
understand that having courage is God-given. Having courage to
fight for our Father, to fight for our brothers and sisters, is given
through the Spirit of God. The same Spirit that lives in him is alive
in us—that thought alone must push us.

Second Timothy promises us that our spirit gives us power, love, and
self-discipline. In order to see the fullness of God's Spirit, we need
to take a step. It doesn't need to be a full-blown jump—just a single
step to ignite a flame. A step might be taking a colleague to coffee,
asking your waiter if they belong to a church, or reaching out to that
neighbor you've always wondered about. A step is powerful; it can
plant a seed the size of a mustard seed. And that same mustard seed
can move a mountain, further his kingdom, and glorify his purpose.

What does stepping out and joining the fight look like for you?

A Found Love

I will show my love to those who passionately love me.
For they will search and search continually until they find me.

PROVERBS 8:17 TPT

God is mysterious and all encompassing. He is much bigger and more powerful than we can begin to understand. And yet, he doesn't hide himself from us. Not only is he present in our lives, he is patiently waiting for us to come to him. He is waiting to love on us. He wants us to know him in the same capacity that he knows us.

In order to search for him we need to slow down our busy bodies and minds, sit still in his presence, and listen carefully to him. When life is so busy, and full of so many things, it takes a great deal of discipline to carve time out in our day just to focus on our relationship with God. He is always there, always present, but sometimes we are too distracted to notice. It is in the quiet places that we are able to see him, feel him, and hear him. When we set our hearts out to search for him in these places, when we desire to know him intimately, and begin to look for him in everything, he reveals himself to us.

Are you satisfied in your relationship with God?
Do you desire to know him more intimately?

Crown of Beauty

To all who mourn in Israel, he will give a crown of beauty for ashes,
a joyous blessing instead of mourning, festive praise instead of despair.
In their righteousness, they will be like great oaks
that the LORD has planted for his own glory.

ISAIAH 61:3 NLT

God is so capable of taking something horrible and creating something beautiful. When we are sad, he offers us comfort and joy. He turns our despair into reasons for celebration. In the middle of heartache, we should still seek God and trust him with our problems. He has a knack for mending what is broken.

Ask God to establish you like a strong tree so when distress comes upon you, you will not crumble. He will help you makes sense of the madness and reestablish you once again. Give him your broken heart and let him give you a crown of beauty in exchange.

What might be an accurate conclusion if the Lord does not immediately alleviate your suffering?

Walk Boldly

The Lord is always good and ready to receive you.
He's so loving that it will amaze you—so kind that it will astound you!
And he is famous for his faithfulness toward all.
Everyone knows our God can be trusted,
for he keeps his promises to every generation!

PSALM 100:5 TPT

God's best is yet to come. Don't give up. Trust him. Your past, your worries, your fears can be done away with. He is releasing you into a new phase. He has released joy, peace, and prosperity of your soul over you. Keep stepping out into courage. Keep living in boldness. Keep saying "Why can't I?" He has created you to be a person of power and a person of influence. He trusts you to live out his love. You are a storehouse of peace.

When God speaks something over you, he creates something new in you. He can create new things at any time. Maybe he'll create new levels of courage and boldness in you so you can demonstrate his heart to others even when it feels scary.

How can you step out in courage today?
List the ways God is revealing in this moment.

Ever Thankful

Be thankful in all circumstances,
for this is God's will for you who belong to Christ Jesus.
1 THESSALONIANS 5:18 NLT

God's grace is more than sufficient to carry us through any circumstance. His love is unending and his mercies surround us every day. Understanding how great of a God we serve gives us a reason to be thankful always. Even when we are having difficult days, we should be filled with gratitude for all God has done. Hard times will pass, but God's grace never will.

Our thankfulness is also closely linked to the testimony of what God has done and how we represent the love we have received. When others see us being thankful in every circumstance, they will know that our joy is not dependent on good times but on a good God.

If you truly belong to Christ, how does that change how you approach difficult circumstances?

Loving Arms

Do not be anxious about anything, but in every situation, by prayer and petition, with thanksgiving, present your requests to God.

PHILIPPIANS 4:6 NIV

Grandma Peg usually liked giving Ben a bath. Lathering up his dark hair and wiping his face. Washing those soft, dimpled hands and feet. Pouring suds over wrinkled baby belly and back. Then watching while her grandson splashed and kicked in the warm water. Not this time though. He was overtired and wanted nothing to do with bath time. The crying began when she started the water in the tub. She bathed him as quickly as possible, while tears dripped off his cheeks into the water. When she wrapped him in the fluffy towel, his lavender-scented body relaxed in her arms and he stopped crying immediately. He snuggled deep into Grandma Peg's arms, his eyes getting heavy and his breathing growing deep.

Do you ever wish you could snuggle deep into your heavenly Father's arms? When you just want to lean back and tell him all of your problems and cares and worries. And you just want to be held. Like a child again. With soothing promises that everything is going to be okay. This is available to us at any time. God wants to hold us in his care. To wrap his arms around us in love. To listen to the stresses and cares of the day. To wash away all of our worries and fears. To comfort us and give us hope.

How can your struggles and challenges draw you close to God?

Walk with the Wise

If you want to grow in wisdom,
spend time with the wise.
Walk with the wicked
and you'll eventually become just like them.
PROVERBS 13:20 TPT

Habits and behaviors are learned. We are far more susceptible to influence than we would like to imagine, and the more we associate with foolishness, the sooner we will resemble fools. This does not mean we ought to reject those who do wrong, since Jesus himself sat with sinners and sought out the lost. But we should surround ourselves with those who are also walking wisely because we are bound to become more like them. Influence is powerful, and so we must purposefully decide what we will allow to influence us.

Ask God to bring sense to the confusion around you as you sit in his presence. He imparts his wisdom to those who seek him and he also encourages you to seek other wise people. He can bring those people into your life and give you humility to learn from them if you only ask him.

Do you associate with wise people
in an effort to learn from them?

Proclaiming Faith

*May he give you the power to accomplish all the good things
your faith prompts you to do.*
2 THESSALONIANS 1:11 NLT

Have you ever been afraid of what others will think of you when they learn that you are a Christian? Do you ever worry that people may assume you are some sort of weirdo if you proclaim your faith? It can be hard enough to fit in without giving society another reason to shun you.

Be assured, there is no reason to be afraid! God has given us his Holy Spirit to guide us through tough conversations. Be bashful no more—he has equipped you with all the talent you need to share his love with those around you. There will be some who will laugh, and there will be some who will scorn you for your beliefs. The Lord himself tells us through his Word that we have nothing to fear.

Shake off your timidity! Picture yourself shedding it like a winter coat in the warmth of spring. Are you prepared to share your faith without fear? God has sent his Holy Spirit to give you power when you lack it. Take advantage of it!

Sacred Places

He who dwells in the secret place of the Most High
shall abide under the shadow of the Almighty.
PSALM 91:1 NKJV

Have you ever been awake when you think no one else is? Maybe you had an early morning flight, and you feel you are the only person who could possibly be stirring at that hour. It feels kind of magical, doesn't it? It's like you have an unshared secret.

Regardless of you being a night owl, morning person, or somewhere in between, there is peace that comes with meeting Jesus in secret—when your world has stopped for a bit. You need spiritual food to conquer each day, so make sure you partake of it.

Aren't you glad to spend moments with Jesus? Even a small amount of time with him gives you the courage to face this day with confidence and serenity.

Weary to the Core

If they stumble badly they will still survive,
for the Lord lifts them up with his hands.
PSALM 37:24 TPT

Have you ever been run so ragged that you just didn't know if you could take even one more step? Your calendar is a blur of scheduled activities, your days are full, your every hour is blocked off for this or that, and it's hard to find even a spare minute for yourself. Even your very bones feel weary, and you fall into your bed at night, drained from it all.

There is someone who is ready to catch you when you fall. You might stumble throughout your busy day, but he will never let you hit the floor as you take a tumble. God delights in you! He will direct your every step if you ask him to. He will gladly take you by the hand and guide you.

Are you allowing the Lord to guide your days? Though you
may be weary, he has enough energy to get you through it all.
Hold out your hand to him today and walk
side-by-side with Jesus.

Perfect Translation

It is God who arms me with strength,
and makes my way perfect.
PSALM 18:32 NKJV

Have you ever been stuck for words, lacking the ability to find exactly how to get across your point? We don't always have all the answers and sometimes we just need the humility to admit that we don't get it.

This verse is a good reminder that God is the source of your strength. When you are going through a difficult time or have a tough decision to make, you don't have to rely on your own understanding because it is not perfect. Instead rely on God as your source. He will guide your mind and your heart toward the right thing.

Can you choose to bring your anxieties about your situation to God? Thank him for arming you with his strength and showing you his perfect ways.

Being Trustworthy

A troublemaker plants seeds of strife;
gossip separates the best of friends.
PROVERBS 16:28 NLT

Have you ever been told a secret? Perhaps it is really happy news. A friend is expecting or up for an award. They have shared the news with you but aren't ready to share it with the world. Can you keep that secret? Are you worthy of their trust? How disappointed will they be when they hear their own news passed around? Keeping confidence is surely a way to show someone how much you care and respect them.

Do you love a good rumor? Passing on the newest delicious tidbit seems to travel faster than the speed of light with no regard for truth or feelings of the people involved. Social media is full of innuendo and made up "facts." Gossip is a selfish act. It makes the teller feel important at the expense of others. When we care about someone, we want the best for them. We don't want to hurt them, their reputations, or their feelings. We want to respect their confidences and keep their trust. A wise person learns to control the tongue and keep trust.

Can your friends count on you to keep a secret?

Split-second Judgment

By the grace given to me I say to everyone among you not to think of himself more highly than he ought to think, but to think with sober judgment, each according to the measure of faith that God has assigned.

ROMANS 12:3 ESV

Have you ever felt like you were split-second judged? You had an encounter, it didn't go as planned, and immediately you felt less than ideal. We desire grace for ourselves when we are having a "bad day," but it's so easy to forget to extend that same grace to others. Maybe we've done it for so long that we don't even realize we are doing it.

Here is what we need to remember: we are the same. We are children of the Most High God, precious, beautifully made in his image. We belong to Jesus. Let us ask God to give us hearts to see others for who they are—siblings—and remember they are nothing less than we are.

Have you had a recent encounter where you've judged someone or haven't extended grace? Reflect on the people in your life and your heart toward them. Ask God to give you eyes to see them as he does.

Feasting

You prepare a feast for me in the presence of my enemies.
You honor me by anointing my head with oil.
My cup overflows with blessings.

PSALM 23:5 NLT

You probably aren't physically preparing for battle today, but in the days of these Scriptures, battle was all too common. When facing enemies, it was important to have the right nourishment so you could have the strength to face the fight.

You won't have enemies or probably need to fight, but you do need strength to face the hurdles that will come across your path. Make sure you are nourished by his Word each day so you are equipped for the day.

How does meditating on the Word of God
equip you for the day?

People of Truth

This Book of the Law shall not depart from your mouth, but you shall
meditate in it day and night, that you may observe to do according to all
that is written in it. For then you will make your way prosperous, and then
you will have good success.

JOSHUA 1:8 NKJV

Have you ever met someone who speaks hard-hitting truth every
time you talk to them? They seem to be soaked in the presence of
God, and you know that when you hear them speak, you will be
ministered to by the power of the Holy Spirit through them. These
people echo the heart of God because they study the Word of God.

If we meditate on truth, we will become people of truth. If we
read the Bible constantly, truth will flow out of us—along with joy,
peace and wisdom. Even in our normal conversations we will find
ourselves using phrases that are directly from Scripture. That's what
God wants. He wants his praise and his words to be continually on
our lips—a never-ending worship service to him as we speak.

*Can you allow God's goodness, kindness, mercy, and grace to
flow out of you as you become a person of truth?*

Cycle

To the praise of the glory of His grace, which He freely bestowed on us in the Beloved. In Him we have redemption through His blood, the forgiveness of our trespasses, according to the riches of His grace which He lavished on us.

EPHESIANS 1:6-8 NASB

Have you ever said or done something that you immediately regretted? It just happened: that horrible moment that we replay over and over again. Then, maybe a few days later, something similar happens. Why does this happen? Why can't we exercise more self-control?

Those moments are the vicious cycle of our humanness. Thankfully, through the blood of Jesus Christ and our repentance, we are forgiven, set free, and released of the burden of our mistakes. We are given a clean slate to start over. And some days that gift feels bigger than others. Some days we rely heavily on the grace of our Lord and Savior just to get through the day. And that is okay.

Have you had a "moment" recently? Do you know you are forgiven through the blood of Jesus? Accept his gift; you are forgiven. Forgive yourself and keep moving forward.

Perfect in Weakness

"My grace is sufficient for you, for power is perfected in weakness."
Most gladly, therefore, I will rather boast about my weaknesses,
so that the power of Christ may dwell in me.

2 CORINTHIANS 12:9 NASB

Have you ever taken a personality test to identify your strengths and weaknesses? You probably know if you are an introvert or extravert, whether you are creative or administrative, good at speaking, or great at listening. You probably also know all too well what your weaknesses are. You might be over-analytical, self-doubting, unorganized, or lacking empathy. There are areas in our life that we certainly don't feel proud of!

Paul, on the other hand, says he would rather boast about his weaknesses! Paul knew that his weaknesses made him rely on the power of the Holy Spirit. You may be facing something that you are worried about because it is outside of your comfort zone. Will you consider that God can shine through you as you acknowledge your complete reliance on his Holy Spirit?

It is not really the weakness in which you boast, but rather the power of Christ that is revealed through your weakness. What do you feel weak in today?

A Forever Song

*This forever-song I sing of the gentle love of God overwhelming me!
Young and old alike will hear about your faithful, steadfast love—
never failing!*

PSALM 89:1 TPT

Have you ever turned on the radio and heard a song that instantly brought you back to a particular memory? Clear as day, you can feel the same emotions, picture exactly where you were when you heard it and immediately feel as young as you did in the times you sang it out loud.

Music is a beautiful way for us to create a soundtrack of life, piecing together songs for the years we heard them. Enjoy God's gift of music today. He can put songs in your heart that bring you joy and comfort.

Do you ever feel overwhelmed with God's presence?

Victory

Thank God! He gives us victory over sin and death through our Lord Jesus
Christ. So, my dear brothers and sisters, be strong and immovable.

1 CORINTHIANS 15:57-58 NLT

Have you ever watched one of those movie battle scenes where
the good guys are grossly outnumbered? You wince as the evil army
swoops in with thousands of troops carrying sophisticated weapons.
While the good army has a lot of heart, you know they don't stand
much of a chance. But when it all seems lost, there is that moment
when, out of nowhere, reinforcements arrive in a surge of hope
to assist the good army. Suddenly, they go from losing terribly to
winning victoriously!

Daily, we are engaged in our own battle against sin. Left to ourselves,
we don't have the strength necessary to win the fight. But when it
seems all hope is lost, our reinforcement—Jesus Christ—arrives,
and we gain the strength to boldly obtain the victory over sin. You
may go through seasons in your life when you feel like sin has you
outnumbered. Temptation is great, and you don't feel that you have the
strength to overcome it. But know that you don't have to fight alone.

*Do you know that you have the power of God on your side,
and he has already won against sin and death?*

Undeniable Trust

"Surely I am with you always, to the very end of the age."
MATTHEW 28:20 NIV

Have you heard a personal story that has made you weep? Have you watched as that person overcame undeniable odds and still clung to Jesus? Were you in awe or did you have confidence that you would react the same in a tragedy or difficult situation? Our response to shattered dreams is incredibly important in our spiritual walk. No matter how we feel, our job is to have complete trust and confidence that God is with us, walking right alongside us, holding our hand.

We are called to love him even when it feels like he's not there. We are called to be faithful even when it doesn't feel like he's faithful back. He is. Trusting in God is pleasing to him. He does the rest of the work for us. Isn't that beautiful? We have to let go and trust him in the wake of shattered dreams. God will take our hand and lead us, doing the hard work for us.

Have you had a tough circumstance where you've had to press into God like never before? How did you respond? He wants you to reach out to him in those hard moments. His love is the best remedy.

Offended

See if there is any offensive way in me
and lead me in the way everlasting.
PSALM 139:24 NIV

Have you taken any personality tests, or tried to figure out what type of person you are? We all know people who are the type to speak their minds even if the words come out offensively. Perhaps you are one of those people! Even if you aren't intentionally trying to cause offense, unfiltered thoughts that land as words can end up being hurtful. If this is one of your vices, take an extra second to think before you speak. It can help to switch that filter on that tells you when you are about to say something rude or unkind.

In the same way, if you are prone to being offended, take a look at the heart of the person who said the wrong thing. Were they really trying to hurt you? Offense is hard, whether you are on the giving or receiving end of it, so allow God's grace to enter those situations.

Do you frequently offend people? Are you often offended?
Take your heart and your offense to God so you can
stop the cycle of hurt for yourself and others!

Mighty Oaks

To strengthen those crushed by despair who mourn in Zion—
to give them a beautiful bouquet in the place of ashes,
the oil of bliss instead of tears, and the mantle of joyous praise
instead of the spirit of heaviness.
Because of this, they will be known as Mighty Oaks of Righteousness,
planted by Yahweh as a living display of his glory.

ISAIAH 61:3 TPT

How many thoughts does the human brain conceive in an hour? In a day? In a lifetime? How many of those thoughts are about God: who he is and what he has done for his children? Imagine your own thoughts about life and your thoughts about God weighed against each other on a scale. Likely, it would tip in favor of the many details of human existence.

These temporary details overshadow the one comfort and promise you can rely on: the gospel of Jesus and your eternal salvation. Wipe every other thought away. You are not a weak sapling, limited by inadequate light and meager nourishment. You are a strong and graceful oak. Ashes and mourning and heavy burdens are relieved. The scales tip to this one weighty thought: you are his.

Can you let your thoughts stretch above the canopy of everyday human details to bask in the joy that God has given you everything you need in Jesus?

Procrastination

Those who wait for perfect weather
will never plant seeds;
those who look at every cloud
will never harvest crops.

ECCLESIASTES 11:4 NCV

I don't want to walk in late; I think I'll just go tomorrow. I'm feeling a little tired; I probably wouldn't do my best today, anyway. I don't feel very creative right now. I'll do it in the morning. How often are circumstances ideal? How often do we think we need to wait until they are?

Right now, today, let's choose together to follow the advice of Scripture and decide that a few minutes late is better than absent. Let's acknowledge our collective fatigue, and then do today's version of our best in spite of it. Let's stop waiting for a burst of creativity, attack our projects, and see what happens. Let's honor God—and surprise ourselves at the same time.

What are you waiting for?

September

Even the strong and the wealthy
grow weak and hungry,
but those who passionately pursue the Lord
will never lack any good thing.

PSALM 34:10 TPT

Stimulating Relationships

In fact, we should come together even more frequently,
eager to encourage and urge each other onward
as we anticipate that day dawning.
HEBREWS 10:25 TPT

If we assemble together, it becomes much easier to network and find close companions who will help us do the right thing. We see things more clearly when we bounce ideas off one another, and we usually work harder when we work as a unit. It is beautiful to see people working together under the Lord's hand. Conversely, it is difficult to do any of these things when we remain in isolation.

Note that the concept of forsaking church is juxtaposed with encouraging one another more. When runners are about to cross the finish line, the cheering crowd swells to a deafening roar. So, should we raise a growing cheer for our brothers and sisters in Christ. The end of the race is looming near, and Jesus wills that we all keep running to the best of our abilities.

How have you been encouraged by others,
and what was the effect?

A Star Is Born

The LORD merely spoke, and the heavens were created.
He breathed the word, and all the stars were born.

PSALM 33:6 NLT

If you have ever had the chance to be in a remote location on a clear night, you will know what it is like to look up into the sky and marvel at the magnificent display of stars. It is such a breathtaking view—one that reminds us of the greatness of our God, the one who spoke them into existence.

Do you feel insignificant in God's great world? Remember that God has a perfect plan for this world, and you complete his plan. Lift up your eyes and know that he knows your name and that you are not missing from his plan.

When you think of everything God created,
are you amazed that he cares about a plan for your life?
Can you trust that he is in control?

Created Creatures

O LORD, how manifold are your works!
In wisdom you have made them all;
the earth is full of your creatures.

PSALM 102:24 NRSV

If you have ever watched a nature documentary, you will know what it is like to be fascinated by the creature that is being described. If you are capable of being captivated by one creature, imagine just how much there is to learn about every other creature out there!

This world is an incredible place, teeming with imagination and inspiration. Today is not just another ordinary day. Take some time to notice the extraordinary in what God has created in the living things around you.

Can you take some time today to notice the incredible things God has created? Thank him for the inspiration that noticing beauty gives you.

Ordered Steps

I will instruct you in the way you should go;
I will counsel you with my loving eye on you.
PSALM 32:8 NIV

If you've ever taken the hand of a toddler, you'll know that they are relying on you for their balance. If they stumble, you can easily steady them. This simple act of holding a hand means that you and the child have confidence that they won't fall flat on their face!

In the same way, when we commit our way to God, we are essentially placing our hand in his. He delights in the fact that we are walking with him. Even in the times when we stumble, he will steady our path and give us the confidence to keep walking.

Do you feel like you have stumbled lately, or are unsure of your walk with God? Be confident that the Lord delights in your commitment to him. Accept his hand, continue to walk, and trust him to keep you from falling.

Royalty Protocol

Let us come boldly to the throne of our gracious God.
There we will receive his mercy, and we will find grace
to help us when we need it most.

HEBREWS 4:16 NLT

*I*magine walking into Buckingham Palace, unnoticed and unrestricted, without knocking or announcing yourself, and pulling up a chair alongside Her Majesty, the Queen of England. "I've had such a long day. Nothing has gone right, and now my car is making the strangest noise. Could you help me out?"

Such an image is almost absurd! There is a protocol to seeing royalty—many rules to follow, not to mention the armed guards protecting every side. But there is a royal throne we can approach without fear or proper etiquette. It is without guards, payments, locks, and restrictions. Its occupant is the God of all creation, and he is eager to hear about your day's ups and downs.

Approach the throne, shamelessly pull up a chair, and lift your voice to him. He loves your company. What do you need? Ask him without fear. What gifts has he given? What guidance are you looking for? His wisdom is yours if you will listen.

Belonging

This is how we know that we belong to the truth
and how we set our hearts at rest in his presence.

1 JOHN 3:19 NIV

In a world competing for truths, and voices telling you to own your truth, what can be left to say of knowing anything for certain? Truth has the assumption that there is a right belief, beyond all personal subjectivity and experience. While everything that we experience is a level of truth, there is a greater truth about our lives and existence that can only be found in Jesus.

The truth is this: you belong. In a world where we desperately try to find our place, fit in with certain groups, and share common ground, we can often feel isolated. God's truth is that you are a part of his family, and nothing is going to change that. As you dwell in the reality of your belonging, let your heart find the divine presence of the living God, and let yourself rest in it.

How do you know you belong to the truth?
What truths of this world are competing against
the knowledge of your belonging to the family of God?

Allowed to Enter

Who may worship in your sanctuary, LORD?
Who may enter your presence on your holy hill?
PSALM 15:1 NLT

*I*n ancient Israel, the sanctuary wasn't an easy place to enter. It was a place where the living God dwelled and there were requirements of sacrifice and purification before anyone could enter and be cleansed from sin. In that day, it was a selective process: a question worth considering by King David: "Who can worship in this sanctuary?"

We are so privileged that Jesus now lives within us, which makes us holy enough to be in the presence of God at any time. There's nothing you need to do but let Jesus in. Enjoy the freedom of being in the presence of God today.

How do you most easily enter into God's presence?

City without Walls

The grace of God has appeared that offers salvation to all people.
It teaches us to say "No" to ungodliness and worldly passions,
and to live self-controlled, upright and godly lives in this present age.
TITUS 2:11-12 NIV

In grade school, we had to wait to speak until our hand was raised. The teacher would not call on a single student until she had finished talking. The children could barely wait another second before blurting out the answer. These teachers were wise. They were trying to teach self-control—a valuable life lesson.

Lack of self-control comes in a variety of forms: overeating, spending too much time on the computer or phone, losing our tempers, wasting money, gossiping, and the list goes on. Self-control requires discipline. In order to perfect it, we need to practice and ask God for help. Proverbs 25:28 describes a man without self-control as a city broken into and left without walls. What an easy way to let the enemy in.

Which areas in your life require you to practice more self-control? Who can you be accountable to? Ask for help today in the area of self-control. Bring your weakness into the light and find the help you need in the Lord.

Stand Firm

Be on guard. Stand firm in the faith.
Be courageous. Be strong.
And do everything with love.

1 CORINTHIANS 16:13-14 NLT

In summary of all Paul had written to the Corinthian believers, he recapped his letter in an almost bullet point fashion. We must stay on our guard and keep vigilant because we have a real enemy who desires for us to fail. The devil will try to tempt us and distract us from the call God has placed on our lives. The way we can distinguish lies is by standing firm in our faith and knowing what God says.

Our courage and strength come from God. He is mighty and will always save us, so we do not need to be afraid. The more intimately we know God, the braver and stronger we will be. Everything can be done in love because God is love, and those who follow God will walk in the way of love.

Why is love more important than any other commandment or any other spiritual gift?

Brief and Fleeting

LORD, remind me how brief my time on earth will be.
Remind me that my days are numbered—
how fleeting my life is.
PSALM 39:4 NLT

*I*t can be a sobering reminder that our time on earth will come to an end, and as the years go on it's easier to feel as though our time here really is brief. But this isn't the end; it is only a part of the life that God has in store for you.

Don't get down about how fleeting this life is; it is here to be enjoyed and lived as fully as you can. Just remember that there is more joy that extends into eternity. Approach your day with the knowledge that when this life ends, a new, more joyous one begins. Get fresh perspective for the day ahead. Don't become overly concerned about the small things.

*Can you ask God to give you the capacity to stand back
and know that life is too short to get so anxious?*

Fear

Fear and intimidation is a trap that holds you back.
But when you place your confidence in the Lord,
you will be seated in the high place.

PROVERBS 29:25 TPT

*I*f you live in America, it is impossible not to look at today's date and remember—whether from experience or from hearing about it over the years—one of the darkest days in our history. Thousands of lives were lost in a well-planned terrorist attack, and in many ways, things were never again the same. Air travel, for example, continues to evoke a spirit of fear in many hearts that was previously unimagined.

In the New Living Translation alone, the word fear appears 601 times. Primarily, it is there to remind us to fear God; in doing so, he will abate all other fears. The fear God desires from us is not one of mistrust, but one of respect and awe. If we believe completely in his sovereign power, if we give him all our reverence, how can we fear anything else? If God is for us, there is truly nothing to fear. Hallelujah!

What do you fear? Lay it at the feet of the Lord today, and place your trust in him. Know that no matter what your circumstances, your safety in him is secure.

Build Up

Let us do all we can to live in peace.
And let us work hard to build up one another.
ROMANS 14:19 NIRV

It does not naturally occur to us to work hard for someone else's success. Our selfish natures coupled with the world's agenda entice us to focus on our own achievements. Yet the laws of the kingdom of God are often paradoxical to human tendencies.

God calls us to work hard so that others are built up. We are to make every attempt to live at peace, and we are to dedicate our efforts to ensure others are built up. This is not self-centered living; it requires a Christ-centered focus. It requires humility and an eternal perspective.

Is there someone you can help build up?

Creation Clues

Since the creation of the world God's invisible qualities—his eternal power
and divine nature—have been clearly seen, being understood from what
has been made, so that people are without excuse.

ROMANS 1:20 NIV

It doesn't take much to marvel at creation. Looking up into the
night sky, sitting on a shoreline, hiking through a forest, or watching
a bud begin to blossom, our encounters with nature are many. But we
don't often take the time to truly notice how incredible creation is.

God chose to reveal himself to us in a profound way. He knew that
we would have appreciation for the beauty of nature that surrounds
us. His invisible qualities are represented through something visible.
And we describe it as beautiful, awesome, and perfect. This is God.

*Can you take a look around at God's creation today and dwell
on the quality of God that is represented? Allow yourself time to
reflect on God's divinity and eternal power, and thank him for
sharing it with you in a very real way.*

Many Wonders

Many, O LORD my God, are the wonders you have done.
The things you planned for us no one can recount to you;
were I to speak and tell of them,
they would be too many to declare.
PSALM 40:5 NIV

*I*t is good to give God the glory for all the things that we find too wonderful for words. We know from the Bible that God has acted powerfully on many occasions to preserve his chosen people. We know that Jesus performed spectacular miracles. The Holy Spirit moved mightily on the early church and still shows his power to us today.

Remember today the many wonders God has done in your life and in the lives of others around you. Thank him for the interest he has shown in you and for the constant revelation of his goodness and love.

*How can you use the strength you have
found in God to get through each day?*

Saved by Grace

God is so rich in mercy, and he loved us so much,
that even though we were dead because of our sins,
he gave us life when he raised Christ from the dead.
(It is only by God's grace that you have been saved!)

EPHESIANS 2:4-5 NLT

It is important to distinguish that the difference between Christians and people who are unsaved only exists because of what God has done. When we were spiritually dead because of our sin, it was God who gave up his life and covered us with his grace and mercy. Salvation is not by our merit; we choose to accept it.

May this awareness go with you as you engage with others who hold onto their sinful ways. Your freedom was not achieved by your strength; you needed a Savior. Extend grace rather than judgment. Show love when others act unlovingly. Never forget the destitute places you came from.

How can you treat others with grace today?

Devoted to Integrity

Joyful are people of integrity,
who follow the instructions of the LORD.
Joyful are those who obey his laws
and search for him with all their hearts.

PSALM 119:1-2 NLT

It may seem that following a lifestyle contrary to God's instructions will bring joy and satisfaction, but it will not. Our hearts were crafted to desire God. Even if it is the more difficult option with less immediate gratification, following God gives us true fulfillment. We embrace our purpose when we choose to follow God rather than our own whims and ambitions.

People of integrity are known for being honest, dependable, and self-controlled. They are not led around by cultural pressures; they are devoted to God's instructions which give them a framework to follow. The Lord's laws give them joy because they long to serve him with their whole hearts.

What Biblical values do you struggle to uphold?

No Island

Let the peace that Christ gives control your thinking,
because you were all called together in one body to have peace.
Always be thankful.

COLOSSIANS 3:15 NCV

*I*t seems to be that just the right person may come along and alter our point of view to the better. The whispers of a friend to soothe our hearts, the inspiration of a message, the encouragement of a teammate: these all are building blocks of unity and opportunities to grow and share peace.

In Psalm 133, David rejoices in how good it is to experience unity within the church. The Israeli church is a family, so their unity was more pronounced. But make no mistake: we are both grafted into the eternal faith and enjoying the adoption of that family as believers. How great is our peace when we come forward, as called, into the unity of Christ with God?

Has someone helped you change your perspective recently? Can you open yourself up to receive that more often?

Unnumbered Thoughts

How precious are your thoughts about me, O God.
They cannot be numbered!
I can't even count them; they outnumber the grains of sand!
And when I wake up, you are still with me!

PSALM 139:17-18 NLT

It's bedtime and you are ready. Those millions of thoughts spinning wildly all day make a few sluggish cycles. Tomorrow can wait. Your pinhole of consciousness closes like a camera aperture. You sink in blissful oblivion. But waking up is a different matter. How we fall asleep doesn't guarantee how we awake. Sometimes our dawn comes long before the hour it should. Sleep won't return and night hasn't produced its hoped-for rest. Minds take up the gerbil wheel of neverending tasks. Weariness sets in before the day begins.

Psalm 139 is one of the most beloved psalms of King David. It declares an ever-present God, a perfect bedtime reminder of his sovereignty over events, a calming security to end each day, and an important morning truth. David speaks with absolute assurance. His words steady his readers, proclaiming God will never leave us. His thoughts about us outnumber the sand. His intimate surrounding wraps us like a warm embrace.

How does God show he cares for you?

Crucified for you

I am a worm and not a man,
scorned by mankind and despised by the people.
PSALM 22:6 ESV

It's hard to imagine that after all of Jesus' miracles and teaching, people still wanted to crucify him. He didn't come in violence or arrogance, yet he was still despised by many.

Despite all the rejection, Jesus was victorious. Be encouraged if you are facing challenges today that while people may reject you for no good reason, you can be victorious. Stand tall and be proud of who you are in Christ. Thank him that he understands rejection. He can help you in your low points during the day to take courage that your confidence comes from him and no one else.

How can you be victorious despite any rejection you face?

Loss of Control

My flesh and my heart fail;
But God is the strength of my heart and my portion forever.
PSALM 73:26 NKJV

The last number she saw the needle pass on the speedometer: 120. In one blinding instant, the wheels screeched, the glass broke, the pressure increased, the pain surged. All she could see was light and dark—flashes and fear. All she could hear was the deafening silence. And all she knew with certainty was that she had lost control.

Have you ever had a moment where you've felt completely out of control? A car accident, a diagnosis, or some other frightening moment? There are instances in our lives when our own flesh fails us. We recognize in a flash that we are no longer in control of our own outcome—and it terrifies us. In that moment, when control is lost and fear overcomes, there is one thing we can know for certain. He is our strength; God never loses control. When your life, and the outcome of it, is ripped from your hands, it's still resting firmly in his grasp. He is our portion. He is our ration. He is enough.

How can you release yourself today into the control of the only one who will never lose control?

Treasure in Jars

We are like common clay jars that carry this glorious treasure within,
so that the extraordinary overflow of power will be seen as God's, not ours.
2 CORINTHIANS 4:7 TPT

Jars of clay are delicate. They are made from the soil under our feet and molded with water. Clay is not an extravagant or costly material. It is dull and lacks luster. Clay jars break and crumble easily under the pressure of a strong hand. They are vulnerable to elements like heat and rain.

We are jars of clay. Sometimes we embark on situations feeling like we are inadequate, incapable, and weak. The truth is that without the power of God in our lives, we are fragile, easily broken, and destroyed. But still God chooses us. He chooses us in our weakness, in our fragility, and in our shortcomings. He chooses us despite our flaws and imperfections. We are more than dirt and dust, more than molded clay when we have God in our lives. It doesn't matter what comes our way to fracture or shatter us; he makes us unbreakable. We remain intact and he gets the glory.

*Do you know how strong and valuable
the treasure of Jesus Christ is in you?*

A Good Lord

"If people want to brag, let them brag
that they understand and know me.
Let them brag that I am the Lord,
and that I am kind and fair,
and that I do things that are right on earth.
This kind of bragging pleases me," says the Lord.

JEREMIAH 9:24 NCV

*J*esus is the Lord. He came to take our infirmities. He knows what we need, and he knows what we want to do with our lives even better than we know ourselves. Why? Because he has planted wholesome desires in our hearts.

Jesus is also kind. He wants us to know that. He wants us to come to him. We should not hesitate to learn of him, to dwell in him and become one with his intentions. His intentions are always good. He is a kind, fair, and just master. Nobody has room to brag except to know that they should draw near to him and learn of him. That is a good thing to know and talk about to others. When you do, other people will come to know him as well.

*Do you know that your invitation to serve God is as open
as your invitation to receive him and rejoice in him?*

Greater Will

"I can do nothing on my own. As I hear, I judge, and my judgment is just, because I seek not my own will but the will of him who sent me."

JOHN 5:30 ESV

Jesus was divine, and yet in his humanity, he acknowledged his utter dependence on his heavenly Father to guide his every step. Jesus did what the Father wanted him to do, and because he was so sure of God's will he was able to confidently carry out his purpose on earth. We are not Jesus, but we are like Jesus! When he went back to the Father, Jesus promised to leave us a helper that would guide us in the same way that he was guided by the Father.

We have the Holy Spirit within us, and we, too, can be confident that God is able to achieve his purpose in and through us. As you head into the day, or the week, ahead, make it your intention to hear what God might be saying to you. Let him show you his will in the conversations that you have, in the decisions that you make, in the work that you do. You don't have to do it alone!

What do you need to seek Jesus about right now?
Rely on the helper that Jesus promised you.

God's Purposes

I know that You can do all things,
and that no purpose of Yours can be thwarted.

JOB 42:2 NASB

*J*ob knew the Lord. He was a faithful and blameless servant of God who was upright in the eyes of his friends, his community, and even God himself. When he questioned the Lord's intentions, God revealed more about his holy character through a divine dialogue. As righteous as Job was, he was nothing compared to the goodness of God, and he knew that.

Job's response to the revelation was humble and submissive. He had been reminded of who he served and that his pain was not without a purpose. His concluding declaration was that God could do anything, and nothing could oppose God's purpose. No matter how upsetting or intrusive God's plans may feel to us, only he can see the bigger picture. We can trust him.

How did God use Job's suffering for good?

Is Anybody Listening

Listen to my instruction and be wise.
Don't ignore it.
PROVERBS 8:33 NLT

Kate had burned the candle at both ends for months. In the middle. On the top. And underneath. With new contracts at stake for her business, she'd carried her usual workload and added countless hours of labor to prepare for her meetings with potential clients. She'd also volunteered for a variety of things at church and in the community. They were all good things, but they weren't all God things that he had chosen for her to do.

The day came when her body said, "I've had enough. There's nothing left." Kate had no choice but to listen this time. The all-over weakness and the tremble in her legs left her unable to do anything. The dizziness and weird heartbeat scared her. She'd pushed herself to complete exhaustion and there were consequences to pay. Over the next few weeks, Kate made some important discoveries: when God nudges our bodies to yell at us, we'd better listen. A woman who listens to God's instruction and doesn't ignore it is truly wise.

When was the last time you pushed your body past the limit?
How did that affect you physically, spiritually, and emotionally?

Nobody's Perfect

Whoever keeps the whole law but fails in one point
has become accountable for all of it.
JAMES 2:10 ESV

Let's say you have a teenage daughter, and you're leaving her home alone. You trust her, but just so there are no misunderstandings, you leave her a list of no's: no parties, no boys in the house, no cooking with fire, no announcing on social media that you're home alone. Let's say she invites her boyfriend over. Even though she followed most of your instructions, she still broke the rules. Bring on the consequences.

God's law is no different, and that is why we need Jesus. Mess up one command? We've broken the rules. Bring on the consequences. Or…admit what he already knows. We aren't perfect. While we may never kill or steal or eat the wrong thing on the wrong day, we are entirely likely to covet, to take the easy way out, to gossip. Because of grace we get to choose: follow all the rules, or accept his forgiveness in advance.

What do you choose: your ability to keep every command,
or God's grace? Spend some time thanking him for his
incredible, undeserved gift of grace.

Sound of Laughter

We laughed and laughed, and overflowed with gladness!
We were left shouting for joy and singing your praise.
All the nations saw it and joined in, saying,
"The Lord has done great miracles for them!"

PSALM 126:2 TPT

Laughter is one of the greatest sounds in the world. An old married couple dancing. A toddler being tickled. A pair of best friends sharing a joke. When you hear laughter, you can't help but crack a smile yourself.

Imagine what God must feel when he hears his children laughing, singing, and praising him together. Imagine what happiness must sound like to him. Picture a room full of believers singing in harmony to show their love for him. What a joyous, beautiful sound that must be!

How would you feel if you began your day laughing with God?

Not Envious

Don't worry about the wicked
or envy those who do wrong.
PSALM 37:1 NLT

Life is not fair and there are certainly many people who you could think of who are doing better than you in terms of their relative success. The Bible tries to teach us about the true meaning of success. It is not wealth, fame, or status that will bring you true joy.

It is easy to be envious of those who have these things though. When you see others seemingly getting ahead in life, you begin to fret about where you are at. Don't fall into the trap of comparing yourself with others; instead, thank God for the good things he has already provided you with.

How can you turn your complaints into thankfulness?
Even if others seem to be doing better than you are,
try to see that your concerns won't bring you life.
Instead be thankful for all you have.

The Spirit Is Willing

I know that nothing good dwells in me, that is, in my flesh;
for the willing is present in me, but the doing of the good is not.
ROMANS 7:18 NASB

Lord, I know the right thing to do, but I just don't have the strength to do it. This thought has likely been on our minds more often than we want to admit. We don't like to acknowledge that sometimes we just don't have it in us to make the right choice.

Paul understood the internal conflict that we face in doing right. As new creations in Christ, we have in us the desire to do good; however, as part of a fallen world, we are inherently selfish. In which direction do we position ourselves? We can dwell on our desire to do right, or on our desire to please ourselves. The more we set our minds in the right direction, the easier it will become.

*Above all, remember that it is the enabling power of Christ
that you must rely on to continue to make the right decisions;
it is through his grace that you can overcome.
Do you know the right thing to do?*

The Greatest Drama

Come and see what God has done,
his awesome deeds for mankind!
PSALM 66:5 NIV

Many times in the Psalms, the author's inspiration comes from looking back at the stories of old, recalling with joy how their people were able to overcome hardship and be released into a place of freedom. It is the Lord that has sustained and directed these stories. The author credits the Lord, and calls people to come and witness what he has done.

Do you have stories from your family of God's goodness? Perhaps you are in the middle of making your own story that will be told for generations to come. Be encouraged in your hardship. God will bring something good out of it!

Are you afraid to go through hard times? Do you resist being tested or tried? Think of the stories of God's people who went through difficulties but eventually could say that God had done awesome things for them.

October

"In repentance and rest is your salvation,
in quietness and trust is your strength."

ISAIAH 30:15 NIV

Strong and Courageous

Be strong and courageous! Do not be afraid and do not panic before them.
For the LORD your God will personally go ahead of you.
He will neither fail you nor abandon you.
DEUTERONOMY 31:6 NLT

Moses bequeathed leadership of Israel to Joshua in the presence of all the people. He commanded them all to be strong and courageous. If God was on their side, they could not be overcome. Victory would be the Lord's and all strength was his.

When we are confronted with problems too immense for us to handle, we need to ask ourselves if fighting is what the Lord wants us to do. If it is, then he will go before us and provide a way. There is no need for fear or panic when we are following God. He will never abandon us and his plans will never fail.

Have you ever confronted an obstacle seemingly too difficult
for you to overcome, and yet conquered it by God's grace?

No Condemnation

Straightening up, Jesus said to her, "Woman, where are they?
Did no one condemn you?" She said, "No one, Lord."
And Jesus said, "I do not condemn you either.
Go. From now on sin no more."
JOHN 8:10-11 NASB

Most of us know the story of the woman caught in adultery. One of the intriguing moments was when Jesus was questioned about whether or not the woman should be stoned. His response is to stoop down and start writing in the dirt. Jesus' action of stooping in the dirt literally defines one interpretation of the word grace.

As they all stood casting judgement, Jesus removed himself from the accusers, stooping low and occupying himself elsewhere. It spoke volumes about his lack of participation in the crowd's judgement. Because of Jesus' distraction, the eyes of the onlookers were drawn off the woman, perhaps lifting a portion of her shame. With their attention focused on Jesus, he said the words that saved the woman's life: "Let him who has never sinned cast the first stone." One by one, the accusers walked away.

Can you see that Jesus is the only one qualified to condemn you, and he chose to condemn himself instead? You are free and clean because of the grace of Jesus Christ.

Mountain Mover

What then shall we say to these things?
If God is for us, who can be against us?
ROMANS 8:31 ESV

Mountains in creation are awe inspiring, beautiful and majestic. Mountains in our lives are a different story. We often liken our troubles to mountains because of their looming nature, their size, and even the treacherous manner it takes to cross them. Faith allows us to see how much larger God is than our mountains. We stand at the base in disbelief. But faith zooms us out to a view that shows us that though there might be ranges of mountains in our future, God is more expansive than even the atmosphere that surrounds them.

Our focus has to be on how big God is. A lack of faith has an awful tendency to glue our feet to the ground, so we are unable to see anything but negativity. Those who walk in faith are people who admit they might not know how the mountain will be moved, but that God will supply no matter what. He is the mountain mover. Pray for faith to arise, to see how big God is.

What mountains are you facing now? Can you believe that God can move the mountain or help you climb it?

Sleep Isn't Enough

Each time he said, "My grace is all you need.
My power works best in weakness."
So now I am glad to boast about my weaknesses,
so that the power of Christ can work through me.
2 CORINTHIANS 12:9 NLT

No matter how much Lynn rests or sleeps, it's never enough. With rosy cheeks and a bright smile, she looks healthy as can be, but sometimes looks can be deceptive. Lynn has multiple chronic health issues. None of these things are visible to the naked eye, but they're apparent to her on a daily basis. Where many people get six or eight hours of sleep and wake up the next morning refreshed and energetic, Lynn often wakes up feeling as if she hasn't even been to bed.

That sort of fatigue and pain can lead to depression and despair, but you'd never know it by meeting Lynn. Her sweet spirit and smile touch everyone she meets. She has learned that God's grace is enough for the difficult days. Her testing times have become her testimony. Lynn has that even when she doesn't understand why she has to deal with fatigue and pain each day, she can trust the one who knows what's best.

How can you rest in God through difficult days?

Free My Soul

Free me from my prison,
and then I will praise your name.
Then good people will surround me,
because you have taken care of me.

PSALM 142:7 NCV

Nobody likes the thought of being stuck in something they can't get out of. You don't have to have been in prison or trapped in an elevator to know what it would feel like to not be in control of your freedom. These days, we probably feel a little more like we are trapped in a job or mental illness, or maybe we are even trapped by our own sin.

The truth is that Jesus came to set you free. He does not want you to be in a prison of any description. When you ask for a breakthrough, expect freedom, and then be ready to encourage other believers with what he has done for you.

Have you asked Jesus to free you from your prison lately?

Steady Hearts

They won't be afraid of bad news;
their hearts are steady because they trust the LORD.
PSALM 112:7 NCV

None of us like to receive bad news, but we do not live in dread of it like those whose security is shaky. Our hope is rooted in our steadfast Lord, and our confidence comes from knowing him. We cannot secure our own futures nor the results of certain circumstances. In the end, we know the final conclusion of all things is our victory through Christ.

God knows the future and has a perfect plan in place. He is not surprised by sudden disappointments; he has been preparing us to handle them. For this reason, we do not live in fear but in freedom. Our hearts are steady because we trust God, and he has given us his peace.

Does your heart feel steady or anxious thinking about what you cannot predict or control?

Rejoice Again

Rejoice in the Lord always.
I will say it again: Rejoice!
PHILIPPIANS 4:4 NIV

Oh, to be ever the optimist! This verse feels like it belongs to those who are able to keep positive in the middle of the worst crises. For the rest of us, however, it might feel like we are capable of failing this always rejoice command on a daily basis. Life just isn't that nice all the time. You might not like your job, you may be in a difficult patch in your relationship, you may just be annoyed at your neighbor or someone at school.

There are endless situations in a mere day that leave us feeling like not rejoicing. So, what are we to do when things seem dull, frustrating, or depressing? Rejoice in the Lord! Yes, turn your focus off yourself, and let your eyes turn toward Jesus. If you start to think of his goodness, grace, and mercy, your heart will slowly but surely find its joy and hope again. Don't despair, rejoice!

What can you rejoice in the Lord for right now?

Nothing Expected

What can I ever give back to God
to repay him for the blessings he's poured out on me?
PSALM 116:12 TPT

One of the gifts the Lord has given us is the gift of grace. He expects nothing from us when he has given us everything. We wrestle, like the writer of this psalm, with how to repay God for the gift of unconditional love.

God does not ask for repayment; he desires devotion. Follow him. Pursue him. He desires a relationship with you above all else and that is attainable if you allow him in. You will find that being devoted to him is the best gift you can give yourself.

How can you walk in step with God
as you go through your day?

The Best Medicine

A joyful heart is good medicine,
but a crushed spirit dries up the bones.
PROVERBS 17:22 ESV

Our emotions have a direct impact on our mental, physical, and spiritual health. When we choose to find joy even in pain and suffering, it has the capability of healing us. When joy infiltrates our hearts, the burden of suffering is lessened. Our pain takes on a different form and loses the ability to overtake every aspect of our life. We can breathe easier, laugh louder, and rest better.

Joy is closer to our reach than we think. It can be found when we mediate on God's goodness and provision in our lives. It can be found when we take the time to count our blessings and cultivate an attitude of thanksgiving. When we reach out our arms to those near us who are suffering, we can find joy in serving and loving others deeply. Joy is contagious, and its healing powers are endless.

Is your heart filled with overwhelming joy? Or is sorrow and misery crushing your spirit and making you sick?

Extent of God's Love

For this reason I kneel before the Father, from whom every family in heaven and on earth derives its name. I pray that out of his glorious riches he may strengthen you with power through his Spirit in your inner being, so that Christ may dwell in your hearts through faith. And I pray that you, being rooted and established in love, may have power, together with all the Lord's holy people, to grasp how wide and long and high and deep is the love of Christ, and to know this love that surpasses knowledge—that you may be filled to the measure of all the fullness of God.

EPHESIANS 3:14-19 NIV

*P*aul's letter written to the Ephesians was a powerful prayer that sprang from his deep desire to see the people living a life that was only achieved with total commitment to Christ. He believed that it was worth the struggle that often came with living this way, because the reward was great.

This letter could've been written to each and every one of us. When we feel Christ's indwelling in our hearts, we can experience true power, and true love.

Have you experienced how wide, long, high, and deep God's love is for you? He wants you to feel it in its fullness. Pray for that today!

Unexpected Strength

Be strong, and let your heart take courage,
all you who wait for the LORD!

PSALM 31:24 ESV

Our lives are full of circumstances that make us feel weak. We are prone to comparisons and sometimes we measure our strength against others. We feel like we are less beautiful, less skilled, less able. But strength isn't always what our human minds are conditioned to think it is.

Remind yourself of Jesus as he carried his own cross, the verbal abuse he took from the crowd, and the pain that he willingly suffered as he was left to die. The acceptance and endurance of pain and the lack of violence and fighting was all a part of Jesus showing courage and strength in an entirely different way than expected. Take courage. You are stronger than you think.

What is the difference between the kind of strength God gives and the strength of the world?

Freedom through Kindness

He is so rich in kindness and grace that he purchased our freedom
with the blood of his Son and forgave our sins.

EPHESIANS 1:7 NLT

What a tremendous price Christ paid to cover the cost of our sins.
He is worthy of our adoration and our allegiance because it is only
through him that we have life anew. He set us free from the claim
our sin had on our lives. His kindness and grace are unfathomable,
and his love continues to guide us every step we take.

By his blood, we can truly live in freedom. Even when we stumble,
we can stand back up and keep pressing on because he has forgiven
us completely. His amazing grace has provided a way for us to join
his family and become his children. He paid a great price for each of
us, and we can gratefully accept his grace. Thank him today for being
your Father and redeeming you.

How are you using the freedom that Christ has allotted you?

Righteous Roads

Cleanse my heart God and let out of it flow pure words and life abundant.
Follow the steps of the good and stay on the paths of the righteous.
For only the godly will live in the land, and those with integrity
will remain in it.
PROVERBS 2:20-21 NLT

Anyone who runs regularly knows it is good to stick the well-lit path. If you are running at night and decide to take a different, unknown way down a dark road, it is more likely not to go well for you. Wisdom says to stay on the well-lit, pleasant paths of the righteous. God has prepared this path for us. He knows every turn and hill along the way. The way becomes familiar through the reading of his Word and asking him for guidance. He has also given us the gift of others who have walked these righteous roads before.

Who do you imitate? Is it the latest influencer, movie star, or your non-Christian friends? Look for the gift of other believers who passionately follow Christ and imitate them. They have walked these roads already, and you would be wise to follow.

Who do you imitate most? Are they godly examples?

Heavenly Home

We are fully confident, and we would rather be away from these earthly bodies, for then we will be at home with the Lord. So whether we are here in this body or away from this body, our goal is to please him.

2 CORINTHIANS 5:8-9 NLT

Paul knew that his home was with Jesus in eternity. He was not suicidal or seeking death; in fact, he was quite the opposite. He knew that his eternal home was secure, and this gave him courage and the desire to please the Lord in his earthly life.

Paul's point was that his true and lasting home was not this one, and that he was ready to be taken home to Christ whenever God decided it was time. Whether in heaven or on earth, his life's purpose was to be pleasing to God.

Does understanding how much more glorious your resurrected body will be give you confidence in this life?

Just Rest

The LORD will give strength to His people;
The LORD will bless His people with peace.
PSALM 29:11 NKJV

*P*icture a season in your life where you were knee-deep in busyness, swallowed in sadness, or buried in exhaustion. Picture that season and how you looked, acted, reacted, and survived. Now picture Jesus. See his face, feel his warmth, envision his smile. Picture yourself back in that same tiresome season, sitting on a chair in your house, desiring to spend time with God but being so extremely tired that you couldn't find the strength. So you sit.

Here comes Jesus walking toward you. You invite him to come closer but are ready with the excuses and reasons for why you have been absent from him. He walks toward you and outstretches his hand. When he reaches you, his hand starts to move toward your head. Gently, ever so lovingly, he pushes your head to the chairback, and whispers, "Rest, Child, just rest."

*Have you encountered a moment with Jesus where you
understood more fully that he gets you to your very core?
He knows your heart. He knows when your soul needs rest.
Let him stroke your hair and sing you a lullaby.*

Dust

He knows our frame;
He remembers that we are dust.

PSALM 103:14 NKJV

*P*raise God that he, the one who has requirements of us, is also our Maker. That means he knows precisely what we are capable of and what we aren't. He will never ask something of us that we can't do. For, as our designer, he has intimate knowledge of our inner workings.

We need not fear that our outer frame is wasting away. We need not be ashamed that we aren't as physically strong as we once were. That is nothing to be ashamed of. It is by design. Are you feeling frail today? Have no fear; you were not asked to have superpowers. With God as your supplier of strength, you will be able to accomplish all that he is asking of you.

*Is there a way that you can embrace your weakness
instead of resisting it?*

Peaceful Friendships

Let us try to do what makes peace
and helps one another.
ROMANS 14:19 NCV

*R*elationships are hard work and sometimes very messy. It takes time and effort to keep them strong and healthy. In difficult relationships, we wonder if it's worth the effort especially if the conflict lies in differences of opinion and a clash of personalities. Our relationships with each other are a priority to God. He cares deeply about how we love and interact with each other, and it grieves him to see fighting and hurt between us. What is important to him should also be important to us.

Keeping peace can be difficult. We need to reach deep down inside to find forgiveness and grace. God knows and understands how complex and difficult relationships are. He asks us to work on them anyway. We have him to look to as an example. Our words are powerful. They can be used as a tool for peace and encouragement or as a weapon to cut down or cause turmoil and pain. If we are willing to use our words to build each other up, and focus on instilling love and value, we are glorifying God and pleasing him.

Is there anyone in your life today that you could extend love, forgiveness, and peace to?

God's Handiwork

We are God's handiwork, created in Christ Jesus to do good works,
which God prepared in advance for us to do.
EPHESIANS 2:10 NIV

Salvation is not given to us because of our good works, but by
it we can accomplish good works. God calls us his handiwork or
workmanship or artwork. He designed us carefully and intentionally
with a plan in mind for each of us. Good works are the result of
salvation, not the other way around.

God has laid out a plan and a purpose for each of us. There is
no need to try and copy someone else's calling because God has
something more fitting in mind. We only need to trust him and
follow his leading, and everything will be revealed in its timing.

Do you recognize that you are God's artwork,
masterfully crafted for the purpose of bringing him praise?
How were you uniquely created?

A Strong Weapon

A man without self-control
is like a city broken into and left without walls.
PROVERBS 25:28 ESV

Self-control is a powerful weapon. It keeps us from stepping into harm, from becoming entangled in sin. It helps us make wise decisions. It allows us to pause, to wait upon the Lord. It is a tool that God has graciously given to us, so we can be strong and protected in difficult in situations. Without self-control we open our hearts and minds to destruction and chaos. We will repeatedly stumble and fall. We become slaves to our fleshly desires. We are stripped of everything that makes us stand strong and protected.

We don't have to be enslaved to our impulses and chained to temptations and whims. We do not have to let our emotions and desires control us. We are given complete power and complete control. We are victorious against our impulses. When we seek self-control in our lives we become empowered to live a righteous and holy life for God. It is essential to living a life of freedom in him.

Do you feel trapped by your impulses and emotions?
Don't be discouraged or overwhelmed, you have been
graciously given tools and the power to overcome.

Clean Hands

Those who do right will continue to do right,
and those whose hands are not dirty with sin will grow stronger.
JOB 17:9 NCV

Sin disguises itself as freedom, but it is a burden. Sin is a bondage that can pull down the strongest of us. The Lord is stronger, however, and he teaches us how to overcome sin. His Word is a guide and he fills us with power to endure. Although the will to do wrong feels overwhelming at times, the power to do what is right has been put in us; we simply need to learn how to use it.

When we are faced with an opportunity to sin, and we exercise the power to choose instead to do good, we grow stronger. Every sinful ploy that we cast down increases our competence and our confidence. As we learn to respond in the power of God, and habitually say no to sin, our strength increases and it becomes easier to do good.

Is there a sin that you feel powerless to prevent?

Jaws

Be gracious to me, O LORD;
See my affliction from those who hate me,
you who lift me up from the gates of death.

PSALM 9:13 NASB

Some days you just feel like the world is against you. Maybe you ran out of coffee or hot water for your shower. The weather might have turned bad just before you went out for your morning walk. You might have ended up yelling at your family and everyone left the house mad.

Each thing that goes wrong seems to add a little more salt to the wound. This is where you need the healing power of God's grace to soothe the pain of emotional and mental affliction. Call out to him this morning and watch him pull you safely away from the angry jaws of despair.

*Do you feel confident that God will always come to your
rescue? Can you trust him to relieve your pain
and encourage your heart?*

Crowned Victory

The LORD takes delight in his people;
he crowns the humble with victory.

PSALM 149:4 NIV

Some of the most substantial and ultimately wonderful changes in our lives come from moments of vulnerability. But vulnerability takes one key ingredient: humility. And humility is not easy.

Isn't it sometimes easier for us to pretend that conflict never happened than to face the fact that we made a mistake and wronged another person? It's not always easy to humble ourselves and fight for the resolution in an argument—especially when it means admitting our failures.

How can you show grace for people in your life who have wronged you? How can you humble yourself when you have wronged others?

He Hears

If we know that he hears us in whatever we ask,
we also know that we have obtained the requests we ask of him.

1 JOHN 5:15 TPT

Sometimes it can feel as if God is far away: an elusive man in the heavens who is so far above us that surely he cannot be interested in our day-to-day lives. Our desires and requests seem so small by comparison that it seems unworthy a task to even ask him for help.

But he is a God who loves his children. He wants us to be happy, to feel fulfilled. When we approach him with our wants and needs, he truly hears us! The next time you feel as if your requests are too unimportant to bother God about, remind yourself that he is always listening. Though he may not answer you in the way you expect, he is right there beside you, ready to lend an ear.

Allow yourself to be filled with God's presence today. He loves you and wants the best for you. Do you believe that if you ask in his will, he will answer you?

Fear or Fright

Fear of the LORD is the foundation of wisdom.
Knowledge of the Holy One results in good judgment.
PROVERBS 9:10 NLT

Sometimes we think of God as being full of fire and brimstone, doom and gloom. We learn that we should have a fear of the Lord, and suddenly our God becomes a scary one.

There is a significant difference between a healthy fear and being afraid. Though we commonly associate the words fear and fright with one another they don't mean the same thing. Having a fear of the Lord means we respect him. It means we are in awe of him. He is, in fact, a God of great joy. When we seek to be fully in his presence, we can find that joy.

The Father wants you to experience his joy! Pleasures forevermore? Sign up for that! Shake off any old notions of dread or apprehension you may feel about being in his presence, and seek the path of life he has set for you. He is a source of great delight! Rejoice in that knowledge today.

Move Forward

Leaving the elementary teaching about the Christ, let us press on to maturity, not laying again a foundation of repentance from dead works and of faith toward God, of instruction about washings and laying on of hands, and the resurrection of the dead and eternal judgment.

HEBREWS 6:1-2 NASB

Sometimes, we are so wrapped up in rehashing what we have already heard under the guise of "rightly dividing the truth" that we waylay ourselves out of our purpose and goals. We do not need another Bible study or support group to move forward in our walk. We need to get real with Jesus and let him get real with us.

What do you know you should be doing, instead of looking for an enlightened viewpoint on a well-covered topic? Where are you in need of growth for maturity? Where did you stop obeying a command of God in order to placate a person or take a detour? These are hard questions, but they are fruitful if we pursue them to gain maturity and responsibility in our walks. We are not held back by what is outside of us. We are released to progress by our convictions set in motion.

What has freed up in your life as a result of renewing your focus on the Lord and your personal progress?

Empty Stares

Their insults have broken my heart,
and I am in despair.
If only one person would show some pity;
if only one would turn and comfort me.

PSALM 69:20 NLT

"Sticks and stones may break my bones, but names will never hurt me." It's not true, is it? The raw pain of an insult can almost be worse than a broken bone. You will know what it feels like to be accused of things you haven't done, or even worse, be made to feel ashamed for things that you have done.

You can probably think of a time when you made a mistake and others were there to ungraciously point out that mistake. It's such a relief when you find that one person who will reach out with grace and comfort you. Be thankful, today, for those people in your life who you know would be the ones to stand up for you in your times of greatest shame.

*When you feel embarrassed or guilty, can you draw upon
God's grace that releases you from shame?*

True Strength

Fools give full vent to their rage,
but the wise bring calm in the end.
PROVERBS 29:11 NIV

*S*trength is valuable and highly sought after. We admire strong people and aspire to be the strongest versions of ourselves. We invest in gym memberships and self-help courses. We look up to people who are outspoken and boisterous in the face of opposition. But what is the true definition of inner strength? It is much more than our muscle mass and confidence level. True strength can only be found in the character of God. He is mighty but he also gentle. He is kind and slow to anger.

Most often strength comes in the form of gentleness. It comes from the way we interact with people, especially those who are difficult to be around. Often gentleness requires a great deal of self-control and empathy. It asks us to hold our tongues and extend grace. It is often much harder to be gentle than it is to be the world's version strong. However, when we set our hearts to be like God, we are strong through our gentleness.

How can you exercise self-control
and see every person the way God does?

Temper Tantrums

What is causing the quarrels and fights among you? Don't they come from the evil desires at war within you? You want what you don't have, so you scheme and kill to get it. You are jealous of what others have, but you can't get it, so you fight and wage war to take it away from them.

JAMES 4:1-2 NLT

Temper tantrums are as common for adults as they are for children; they just look different in action. Children haven't learned to curb the screaming and stomping of frustration or anger, while adults have more restrained behavior. But the heart is the same, and the reactions stem from the same provocation. We want what we want but we don't have it, so we throw a tantrum. Watch a child and this truth will play out soon enough. Watch an adult, and it may be more difficult to discern, but it is there in all of us.

Praise God for his amazing grace, which is extended to us for this very reason. Let us submit to God's forgiveness and draw near to him for his cleansing and purifying grace. It washes over us, and our tantrums are forgiven. When we humble ourselves, he promises to exalt us. What more could we want?

Do you see responses in yourself that remind you of a child throwing a tantrum?

Healing Words

Careless words stab like a sword,
but wise words bring healing.
PROVERBS 12:18 NCV

Words can cut deeply. Isn't it amazing how many of us struggle to remember a phone number, but we can perfectly recall a string of harsh words spoken to us years ago?

Throughout the Bible, God characterizes a person of wisdom as one of few words. Perhaps this is because a careless word can do so much damage. None of us can deny that words carry power. They can easily leave a mark that is not quickly erased. Do our words bring healing to those around us? We can't underestimate the power of our words. The beautiful thing about this next verse is that it reminds us that wise words bring healing.

Have you spoken careless words lately? You have the power to bring healing with new words of wisdom. If you have been pained by someone else's words, turn to the wisest words ever written—the Scriptures—to bring healing to the scars in your own heart.

Naptime

I'll lie down and sleep like a baby—
then I'll awake in safety,
for you surround me with your glory.
PSALM 3:5 TPT

The baby took forever to fall asleep. The mom was amused as she walked through the room. Her husband was sound asleep, but the baby—held securely in his arms—was bright-eyed and ready to play. On another day, the mother just shook her head as the baby camera caught her toddler in all kinds of shenanigans when he was supposed to be napping. As children become older, it's harder to get them to take a nap even though they really need it. As the teen years arrive, it's almost the opposite. It's all parents can do to drag their kids out of bed by noon, or they nap the afternoon away and then aren't ready to go to bed when nighttime comes around.

Most moms and dads would give anything to swap places and take naps for their children. Somehow that rarely happens. We finally understand the importance of rest and we feel the lack of it. But how can we possibly find the time to rest? God promises rest to his people. He tells us to come and rest awhile. Maybe it's time to listen to our heavenly Father.

Why do you make excuses for why you don't have time to rest?

Run with Endurance

As for us, we have all of these great witnesses who encircle us like clouds. So we must let go of every wound that has pierced us and the sin we so easily fall into. Then we will be able to run life's marathon race with passion and determination, for the path has been already marked out before us.

HEBREWS 12:1 TPT

The believers who walked out their faith before us provide both encouragement and examples to follow. They serve as testimonies of what God can do through people who put their confidence in him.

God does not promise us lives free of pain and difficulty. What he does promise is that he will be with us and give us the strength we need to run this race. You can cast off everything that is hindering you from pursuing him. He will strip your sin and selfishness away and give you endurance to run after him.

Who do you think of as having left a testimony of faith for you to follow?

November

Lord, you are my secret hiding place,
protecting me from these troubles,
surrounding me with songs of gladness!

PSALM 32:7 TPT

Miracles

"Truly, truly, I say to you, whoever believes in me will also
do the works that I do; and greater works than these will he do,
because I am going to the Father."

JOHN 14:12 ESV

The Bible is full of exciting accounts of power, healing, and resurrection. We find ourselves wishing that we had been there when the fire of God fell upon Elijah's sacrifice, or when Lazarus stepped out of the tomb—a dead man alive again.

God is clear that miracles didn't stop when the Bible ended. His power isn't limited by the ages, and he is just as omnipotent today as he was back then—so what is different? Why do we feel like there are fewer miracles today? God tells us that the works he will do through his believers will be greater than the works he did through his disciples. But these works will be done in those who believe. God's power cannot be limited, but his display of power can be decreased by our lack of belief.

*God does not lie. He tells us that by believing in him, we can
and will perform miracles. Can you believe him for something
big, and ask him for it in faith, knowing that he can do it?*

Better Together

God has put the body together, giving greater honor to the parts that lacked it, so that there should be no division in the body, but that its parts should have equal concern for each other. If one part suffers, every part suffers with it; if one part is honored, every part rejoices with it. Now you are the body of Christ, and each one of you is a part of it.

2 CORINTHIANS 12:24-27 NIV

The Bible tells us that God knit us together in our mothers' wombs. Before we were born, our bodies were carefully selected and created by our Maker, ensuring that each part worked with the others to function on the whole. Great care was put into this process.

As Christians, we are all a part of the body of Christ. Just like our physical bodies, if each part is working together with the others, then the entire body functions well and is happy. But if just one part is suffering, the entire body suffers.

What care are you taking to be sure that the body of Christ, your community of believers, is working together? Are you rejoicing together? Look for ways in which you can contribute to the harmony of the body around you.

Today

I will not die but live,
and will proclaim what the LORD has done.

PSALM 118:17 NIV

The conditions Psalm 118 were written in were very bleak. The Psalmist shared about the destitution of his position. With enemies surrounding him and feeling as if he were about to fall, he still wrote that we should be glad and rejoice. Joy is a choice; one we must make in the good times as well as the hard times. It requires action and decision. Our perspective must be bigger than our problems, and our hearts need to stay fixed on God.

By his grace and faithfulness, the Lord has created every day. This alone is reason to thank him and to rejoice. The days belong to the Lord whether they are full of happiness or travesty. We can choose to be grateful and glad, regardless of what we have to face.

What about today makes you glad?

New Life

We died and were buried with Christ by baptism.
And just as Christ was raised from the dead by the glorious power
of the Father, now we also may live new lives.
ROMANS 6:4 NLT

The entire human race is living on borrowed time. We spend our lives with the innate knowledge that we never know when it will all end for us. Death comes, as it always does, to every man.

When it came to Jesus, death didn't have the final say. And in that death—the one death that represented all humanity—the greatest form of life was born. The Gospel truth is that Jesus' death wasn't just a man's life ending on a cross. It was the death to literally end all deaths. Jesus died and took the full wrath of a righteous God upon himself so that our death sentences would no longer be ours to serve. And the story doesn't end there. The most glorious part of all is his resurrection: his conquering of death, and the ultimate display of power, glory, victory, and grace.

The whole point of the entire Gospel, summed up in one life giving phrase is this: you can have new life. This beautiful truth isn't just a charming thought. It's your reality as a Christian. Can you accept the finished story of the Gospel?

The Farmer

You have six days each week for your ordinary work,
but on the seventh day you must stop working,
even during the seasons of plowing and harvest.
EXODUS 34:21 NLT

The farmer pulled his dusty cap from his head and wiped away rivulets of sweat. His hand mixed with the moisture left paths of wet dirt and grime like muddy tracks across his forehead. He held his cap's bill in his big hand then plopped it into place again on the top of his head. He jiggled it a bit back and forth until it fit just right like a bottle-cap back on ketchup. Rest would come after the grain lay safe in big steel bins.

We may not have the same sticky grunge of the farmer in our jobs, but the insistence of those times hits us with the same urgency when projects call, children cry, or looming deadlines arrive. Calendars beg us for space. Time squeezes us for breath. Seasons of our lives will come and go with demands. Some of them simply must be met. But our busyness necessitates time set aside for rest. A vacation, a schedule-cleared weekend, or even an hour in the day for a short nap are blank slates worthy of planned forethought. God himself initiated rest. Surely it must be valid for us as well.

What might you need to change to give space for Sabbath rest?

One Body

Yes, there are many parts, but only one body. The eye can never say to the hand, "I don't need you." The head can't say to the feet, "I don't need you." In fact, some parts of the body that seem weakest and least important are actually the most necessary.

1 CORINTHIANS 12:20-21, 24-25 NLT

The healthiest body is one that takes care of all its members and recognizes the value of each as well. When we are comfortable and confident being who God made us to be, and when we support and encourage others to do the same, only then can we properly function as a body and as a well-designed team.

Thank God for every member of his body. Thank him that under him we are all united for a common goal. We can learn the true value of working with others and treat each person with respect when we operate out of God's love and grace.

What are some skills you do not possess that you are grateful others do? What gifts do you contribute to the body of Christ?

Knit Me Together

You created my inmost being;
you knit me together in my mother's womb.
PSALM 139:13 NIV

The Lord does not make mistakes, and he made each of us. We were intentionally made for an eternal purpose. The actual term David used for inmost being referred to the kidneys. In the days when he penned these words, the kidney was esteemed by the Hebrews as being where our desires and yearnings were born. So, David is attributing our deepest and most primary desires to God as author and creator.

We were carefully knit together by God, including our desires, character, and all other unique qualities. Instead of sacrificing our desires on the altar of adherence, we should ask God to reveal his plan for why he created us the way he did. He has a specific plan for each of us.

What are some of your God-given desires?

Cheerful Giver

Each of you should give what you have decided in your heart to give.
You shouldn't give if you don't want to.
You shouldn't give because you are forced to.
God loves a cheerful giver.

2 CORINTHIANS 9:7 NIRV

The Lord repeatedly makes it clear that is it not the religious rituals that move his heart, but the joy his children experience from following him. He wants our hearts, not our actions. Grateful and cheerful hearts will desire to do good and live generously. At that point, it is no longer simply a Biblical obligation, but a privilege and a delight.

God has plenty of wealth. He can address every need himself, but he chooses to use us as participants in his plan. This is an honor not to be taken lightly. It should overwhelm us with gratitude and cheer.

How does giving benefit the giver as well as the receiver?

Unfolding of Words

The unfolding of your words gives light;
it gives understanding to the simple.

PSALM 119:130 NASB

The more familiar we become with the Scriptures, the more our understanding matures. The Bible is intended to be understood by everyone, from the scholar to the simple. We just have to decide to dedicate ourselves to its study and ask the Lord for wisdom.

Through the Word of God, we learn how we originated, what God's ultimate plan for our futures is, who we are, and what we were created for. Without God's insight, we are left to confusion and darkness. Rather than pursuing ourselves and temporary happiness, we should pursue our God-given purpose.

What has God revealed to you lately through the Scriptures?

Our Strength

> Even though the fig trees have no blossoms,
> and there are no grapes on the vines;
> even though the olive crop fails,
> and the fields lie empty and barren;
> even though the flocks die in the fields,
> and the cattle barns are empty,
> yet I will rejoice in the LORD!
> I will be joyful in the God of my salvation!
>
> HABAKKUK 3:17-18 NLT

The pile of bills, the noise the car is making, the layoff rumors at work, the child who stayed home sick—again. Pressures can overwhelm us, especially when they accumulate. Add in the stresses we put upon ourselves—Am I good enough? Why did I say that? Other women's houses aren't this cluttered—and you've got a potent recipe for insecurity.

When things seem impossible, and they often do, praise God that we have his promises and his power. It is not up to us to solve our problems; we need only to trust the Lord and accept his help.

Where could you use a little, or a lot of, God's strength right now? Offer your worries to your Father.

A Quiet Place

Because so many people were coming and going
that they did not even have a chance to eat, he said to them,
"Come with me by yourselves to a quiet place and get some rest."

MARK 6:31 NIV

Have you ever tried to rest in a noisy place or with people constantly running in and out of the room? Jesus and his disciples were in one of those busy environments. There was such a constant stream of people coming and going that they couldn't eat, much less rest. That's when Jesus had an idea. He told them to come with him to a quiet place so they could get some rest. There's something about a quiet place that provides healing—physically, emotionally, and spiritually.

When was the last time you could be still? Where you could rest? Where you could spend uninterrupted time with God? Time with Jesus provides a rest we can't get any other way. The Bible says that our mouths say what's in our hearts. When our hearts are full of turmoil, stress, and anxiety, unkind words will erupt. We'll hurl impatient words at those we love. But when our hearts are full from quiet times with Jesus, his sweetness will overflow in all that we do.

*When was the last time you spent some
quiet moments with God?*

Constant Complaint

Do everything without grumbling or arguing, so that you may become blameless and pure, "children of God without fault in a warped and crooked generation." Then you will shine among them like stars in the sky as you hold firmly to the word of life. And then I will be able to boast on the day of Christ that I did not run or labor in vain.

PHILIPPIANS 2:14-16 NIV

The temptation to complain or bicker can be overwhelming at times. Get a group of women together in a room and you can almost see the tension grow. "She did this and it wasn't fair." "He doesn't contribute the way he should." "My life is hard for a multitude of reasons." The list can go on and on.

Our complaints are often valid and true, but we miss the joy that the Lord desires for us when we seek out only the negative. This letter from Paul to the Philippians was written thousands of years ago, but it could just have easily been written today. We still live in a warped and crooked generation. Let's shine like stars in the sky! Let us hold firmly to his Word as we speak life to those around us.

What complaints do you need to let go of today?

Trust God

In the day that I'm afraid, I lay all my fears before you
and trust in you with all my heart.
What harm could a man bring to me?
With God on my side I will not be afraid of what comes.
The roaring praises of God fill my heart,
and I will always triumph as I trust his promises.

PSALM 56:3-4 TPT

The true battles we fight are not against each other, but against the devil and his lies. Since God has already claimed victory over the devil, the victory is ours now. Yet, still the war continues. Those who have rejected Christ and have bought into the enemy's lies will consequentially reject us because Christ is in us.

Although our enemies may rise up against us, they have no power over us since they have no power over Christ. Even if they were to hurt our flesh, they cannot harm our souls. When we are afraid, we can trust that God is with us.

*How does knowing the Word of God better
and believing it in your heart help to cast out fear?*

Blessed Are the Gentle

"Blessed are the gentle,
for they shall inherit the earth."
MATTHEW 5:5 NASB

The word *gentle* used in this verse is also often translated as *meek*. The Greek word for meekness referred to a war horse that had been tamed. Only the very best horses who were highly akin to their rider's voice and who would listen to his commands even in the heat of battle, were used out on the field. The other horses were used to pull cargo and such.

Gentleness and meekness can be inaccurately understood as weakness. Being gentle before God and attentive to his voice takes focus and discipline. It takes practice, training, humility, and patience. True gentleness is of great value to a believer, and there is nothing weak about it.

*Why would God choose to entrust the earth
to the gentle and meek?*

The Right Rest

"My Presence will go with you,
and I will give you rest."

EXODUS 33:14 NIV

We tend to be expert multitaskers. We juggle many responsibilities, schedules, and details. As the holiday season approaches, these tasks only seem to increase. Between the cooking and decorating, the parties and festivities—we can easily get tired out.

God says in his Word, "Be still and know that I am God." He asks us to stop, to sit, and rest because he designed us to need rest. There is a reason God set the example by resting on the seventh day after he made the world. Even the Creator knew the importance of rest. Have you ever gotten up from the couch and still felt weary—sometimes even wearier than when you sat down? Don't confuse resting your body with resting your soul. True life-giving rest comes only from being in the presence of the Father.

Can you pause within the busyness of the impending holiday season to sit before God, read his Word, and wait on him as you recharge in his presence?

Wellbeing

The human spirit can endure in sickness,
but a crushed spirit who can bear?
PROVERBS 18:14 NIV

There is a clear connection between our emotional and physical wellbeing. The Lord created our bodies to operate as whole units, so to overlook a piece is to be negligent toward the entire thing. The Lord offers joy that is calming and healing. Although many aspects affect our overall heath, having a joyful spirit can offer a great deal of help to our overall wellness.

The Lord designed us to worship him. When we do, we experience his joy and peace because we are fulfilling our purpose. It will be better for our bodies than we could ever imagine. When our hearts are encouraged and we have something to put our hope in, it helps to strengthen and focus our entire bodies.

How can joy help you physically?

Rest in God

> "As the heavens are higher than the earth,
> so are My ways higher than your ways,
> and My thoughts than your thoughts."
>
> ISAIAH 55:9 NKJV

There are days when your activities and thoughts are concerned with the mundane. Will the traffic light stay green? What should we have for dinner? Is there anything in the refrigerator to make dinner? You throw up a quick, "Help me God!" and rush to the next task on your never-ending list of things to do. Busy days rush into tiring weeks, turning into bustling months of preoccupation. It can feel as if we are on an ever-faster spinning carousel, clinging to a brightly painted steed, hoping against hope that we can just hold on. Sound familiar?

God knows your thoughts. He knows the peace your spirit yearns for. He is concerned with eternity while you struggle with this moment. Spending quiet time with the Lord will help you find a perspective that transcends the confines of today's world. He knows the pressures you feel and wants to give you peace. A heart in sync with God will help you to be joyful and serene in chaos.

Are there ways you can prioritize what you need to do
and weed out some things for time with the Lord?

The Right Fuel

It is good to proclaim your unfailing love in the morning.

PSALM 92:2 NLT

There are a number of different fuel options at the pump. A driver can choose from regular, premium, and at some stations, an ethanol-based fuel. All three options will work in most cars, but some vehicles were designed to run best with premium gasoline. The engine will not operate at its optimum on regular gas, and long term it has the propensity to break down sooner.

God designed us not to simply trudge through our days but to thrive. In Psalm 92, he admonishes us to begin our days reflecting on his unfailing love. His intent is that we would be strengthened in our spirits to know that no matter what comes our way, we have been loved with a love that is incapable of failure. Can we function without knowing this? Sure, just like a car on regular gasoline. But we were designed to run on premium, each day remembering that we are loved so we dwell in grace and peace instead of anxiety and fear.

Do you refuel with God's love every day
or trust in something cheaper?

Joyous Journey

Consider it pure joy, my brothers and sisters, whenever you face trials
of many kinds, because you know that the testing of your faith produces
perseverance. Let perseverance finish its work so that you
may be mature and complete, not lacking anything.

JAMES 1:2-4 NIV

There is great joy in the journey: in the mundane details, in the
difficult times, in the confusing moments, and in the tears. There is
so much joy to be found in the quiet and in the noise.

Pity parties and comparisons create a direct path for the enemy to
steal our joy. There is hope in Jesus and the gift of little joy-filled
moments. They come in varying forms: sunshine rays pouring in
the windows, a nice person at the check-out counter, a turn-the-
radio-as-high-as-it-can-go kind of song, a dance party in the living
room, or the taste of a delicious meal after a long day. Whatever the
moment, there is joy if we look for it.

There's a journey of joy in waking up every day
knowing it's another day to breathe in the fresh air.
Can you find joy in the moment today?

Abound in Hope

May God, the inspiration and fountain of hope, fill you to overflowing with uncontainable joy and perfect peace as you trust in him. And may the power of the Holy Spirit continually surround your life with his super-abundance until you radiate with hope!

ROMANS 15:13 TPT

There is nothing worth hoping for in this life, for everything will one day pass away. The only one worthy of all our hope, who can fill us with all joy and peace, is God. Since we know what he has in store, we can face this life now with joy for what is to come and peace knowing that everything will one day be made right.

God sent the Holy Spirit to guide us and rekindle our hope for the age to come. He fills us with power to face any battle because we already have the assurance that we win in the end.

What does abounding in hope mean to you?

Mystery and Hope

Since through God's mercy we have this ministry, we do not lose heart.
Rather, we have renounced secret and shameful ways; we do not use
deception, nor do we distort the word of God. On the contrary, by setting
forth the truth plainly we commend ourselves to everyone's conscience
in the sight of God…For God, who said, "Let light shine out of darkness,"
made his light shine in our hearts to give us the light of the knowledge
of God's glory displayed in the face of Christ.

2 CORINTHIANS 4:1-2, 6 NIV

There is so much mystery to life. So many unanswered questions
and unknowns. Faith in and of itself is a huge element of mystery.
In order to live a faith-filled life, we accept the elements of mystery
because we know what goes hand-in-hand with it…hope. Hope is
God telling us that his purpose is bigger than any unknown. When
we walk through anything, no matter how great a mystery, God is
walking alongside us.

God doesn't promise us an explanation, and therein lies the mystery.
But he does promise his presence, and that is an unfailing truth.
When we walk through deep waters, he is there.

Have you had a moment of mystery?
An unexplained circumstance or situation
that you wish you could ask God about?

Unburdening

Here's what I've learned through it all:
Leave all your cares and anxieties at the feet of the Lord,
and measureless grace will strengthen you.

PSALM 55:22 TPT

This life is always going to hand us some pretty big burdens. We have responsibilities for so many things. You might need to finish an assignment, deliver a work presentation, or take care of a sick child. Sometimes we face even harder burdens like a health crisis or loss of a job. Cares and anxieties are real, yet Jesus wants us to give them to him. What does that mean to you?

Leaving your cares with Christ might simply mean that you have someone to pour your heart out to. It is often said that we unburden by sharing our thoughts and emotions with others. Well, Jesus is ready to hear everything—you don't have to hold back! Spend some time bringing your cares and anxieties to him today.

Can you bring your worries to God and accept his grace
and strength to face the day ahead?

Be-loved

Put on then, as God's chosen ones, holy and beloved,
compassionate hearts, kindness, humility, meekness, and patience.
COLOSSIANS 3:12

This Scripture comes to us after a list of things Paul asks the believers in Colossians to put off or stop doing. When reading this verse, did you fly right past the beginning to the list of things we needed to do? Put on compassion, kindness, humility, and so on? I think most of us rush right past these three little with big meaning found at the beginning of the verse. Read this next part slowly: you are God's chosen one.

You are found Holy in Christ. You are beloved. What does this even mean? It means esteemed. Favorite. Worthy of love. The love we receive from God is not the "scratch my back and I'll scratch yours" kind of love. It's not a love you earn. It's the God who paints sunsets and brings forth life asking you to be-loved. You want to know what might be the bravest thing you do today? Stop working, achieving, and racing, and allow yourself to be-loved by God.

*How can you slow down today to focus on
the truth of being loved by God?*

Wishing Well

May he grant you your heart's desire
and fulfill all your plans.

PSALM 20:4 ESV

This verse sounds like some good words for a well-wishing greeting card! It's great to reflect on the positive words of others because more often than not, we genuinely do wish the best for other people and we do hope that their heart's desires and plans will be fulfilled.

Think of this verse as a prayer for you. May he grant you your heart's desire and fulfill all your plans. Be glad for the friends and family memberw who really do hope and pray good things for your life.

*Can you start your day being encouraged by
God's desire to bless you?*

Faith Is Evidence

*Faith is the assurance of things hoped for,
the conviction of things not seen.*

HEBREWS 11:1 NASB

Those with faith are not expected to cower in fear but to have confidence in the power of God. Hebrews offers testimonies of those who underwent extreme circumstances yet persevered because of their faith. That same faith is accessible to us because the same God rules our hearts today.

We have complete assurance in God and in the unseen things he has promised us. Clinging to this conviction is putting our faith in God. Furthermore, God makes himself evident to the world through our faith.

Why is faith based on conviction and evidence?

Spirit of Power

God gave us a spirit not of fear
but of power and love and self-control.
2 TIMOTHY 1:7 ESV

Timothy had served alongside Paul for quite a while, and 1 Cor 16:10 suggests that he may have preferred to work that way since he was struggling with fear and being intimidated. Here, Paul, the outspoken and gregarious leader, wrote to Timothy to remind him that it is God who puts a spirit of power and self-control in him. He has nothing to fear since he is engaged in the Lord's work.

We are given a spirit of power, love, and self-control, so we need not fear when God calls us to a specific work. We can rely on him to help us stand and do exactly what he wants us to. When we are intimidated or want to hide in the shadows, we can be reminded that it is God who works in and through us. We don't have a spirit of fear because the Spirit of God lives in us and that fills us with power and self-control.

What intimidates you?
Has God asked you to step up or speak up?

Perfect Pillow

Jesus said to him, "Foxes have holes, and birds of the air have nests,
but the Son of Man has nowhere to lay his head."

LUKE 9:58 ESV

Try finding just the right pillow and you will soon discover exactly how spoiled we are. Choices fill the aisles of department stores. Pillow varieties include size, shape, firmness, and materials. Price tags run the gamut from reasonable to outrageous. Each advertise the sleep benefits of their product. For many people worldwide, the hunt for the best pillow isn't an issue. Countless are simply grateful for a place to rest their heads.

In a passage counting the cost of discipleship, Jesus answers an eager follower who believes he is ready to follow the Master anywhere: "The Son of Man has nowhere to lay his head." Jesus' home was a heavenly one. He recognized his belonging didn't come from a house or his own bed. He wasn't concerned about the feathers or foam in his pillow. He wanted his disciples to have the same mindset. This life of work and toil, full of unrest and hardship, will never be our forever home. We are passing through, and there is something much better ahead.

What makes you feel safe and secure at night?

At the Beach

He calmed the storm to a whisper
and stilled the waves.
PSALM 107:29 NLT

There's something about a day at the beach that speaks to our souls when times are hard. The sun warms our bones and relaxes us while a soft breeze blows. Colorful beach umbrellas flap gently in the wind. The ocean stretches out before us in varying hues of blue and green. The whoosh, splash, whoooooosh, splash of the waves breaking on shore lull us into much-needed rest.

Sometimes we forget that the God who stills the waves can also still his children. He loves to see them enjoying life—and he knows that when they are stressed and weary, when their shoulders are weighed down with cares, that spending time delighting in what he's made can refresh them for the days ahead.

What places bring peace and rest to your soul when you are anxious? Have you thought to pray and specifically ask God to let you go there?

You Have Gifts

We have different gifts,
according to the grace given to each of us.
ROMANS 12:6 NIV

We all have something we feel most alive when doing. Call it a hobby, a talent, a passion—our niche. When we find that thing we both enjoy and excel in, it's one of the most special discoveries.

God has created us each with a unique skill set. He blessed us with talents that both distinguish us from others and complement us to others. He gave us these gifts so that we, as a whole created body of believers, could further his purposes and advance his kingdom. Think for a moment about the specific gifts God has given you. Don't be modest—God gives us gifts so that we can be confident in them for his glory!

Think about your gifts in direct relation to the kingdom of God. How can you use your gifts to benefit the church, the community, and the world? Seek to be an active participant in the kingdom of God using the tools that God specifically chose for you.

Potter and Clay

O Lord, you are our Father.
We are the clay, and you are the potter.
We all are formed by your hand.
ISAIAH 64:8 NLT

We are carefully designed for a purpose exactly the way God intended. The Lord does not make mistakes; he makes masterpieces. Before we criticize ourselves, we ought to consider the insult this is to our creator. Rather than focusing on what we lack, we recognize instead our unique design.

While it is honorable to work toward improving our health, minds, and emotions, we should not become disdainful of who we are today. Those who have invited God to be the Lord of their life have the Holy Spirit living within them. They are his chosen temple and are precious in the sight of God.

Do you marvel at how the Lord formed you and praise him for your body, mind, talents, and personality?

December

"Do not be afraid or discouraged,
for the LORD will personally go ahead of you.
He will be with you; he will neither fail you
nor abandon you."

DEUTERONOMY 31:8 NLT

The Word

How can a young man keep his way pure?
By guarding it according to your word.
With my whole heart I seek you;
let me not wander from your commandments!
I have stored up your word in my heart,
that I might not sin against you.

PSALM 119:9-11 ESV

We are met with a lot of opposition in our daily pursuit of Christ. We get sidetracked so easily with the things of this world, our own emotional struggles, and our war with sin. Without the truth of the living, active Word of God, we are defenseless to successfully live the Christian life.

The Word of God is our best defense against hopelessness, fear, and sin—and at the same time it's our best offensive weapon against temptation, lies, and the enemy of our souls.

Can you make a goal for yourself to memorize Scripture that will equip you for daily living? The Word of God is the most useful, instructive, powerful book that you will ever get your hands on. Eat it, absorb it, know it, and live it.

Ability

He trains my hands for battle;
he strengthens my arm to draw a bronze bow.
PSALM 18:34 NLT

We aren't just children of God. We are his warriors, his conquers. That truth can be difficult to embrace. In the face of opposition we wonder, are we capable? Are we equipped? Are we able?

The God who calls us to the front lines, doesn't leave us vulnerable, he doesn't leave us to be bloodied and bruised. He goes before us. He puts weapons in our hands. In the middle of a battle, when we feel we aren't able, the one who battles for us all keeps us grounded. He breathes confidence in our souls. We can stand strong no matter what strength the enemy portrays because ultimately, we are stronger. He has trained us for these very moments.

What battles are you facing today?
Do you know that you aren't fighting alone
and that the battles have already been won?

At All Times

Be joyful because you have hope.
Be patient when trouble comes,
and pray at all times.
ROMANS 12:12 NCV

We cannot fabricate happy feelings, but we can become so acquainted with the hope we have in Christ that it fills us with joy even in our sorrow. When trouble comes, we know that it will not last, so we can persevere patiently. God has assured his victory in the end.

Praying at all times offers the understanding that God is nearby and wants an active role in our lives. By conversing with him, living according to his Word, and taking time to listen for his voice, we can have our joy, hope, and patience renewed daily.

When you feel like you're lacking patience, do you pause ask God to remind you of the hope you possess?

Patience

The Lord is not slow in keeping his promise, as some understand slowness. Instead he is patient with you, not wanting anyone to perish, but everyone to come to repentance.

2 PETER 3:9 NIV

We have instant-everything. The internet is answering questions, giving us directions, and so much more. We can talk or FaceTime people on the other side of the globe in real time. An ATM will dispense cash from our bank at any time of day or night. There is an Instant Pot to cook in, a microwave and fast food for instant dinners. Amazon has opened up an instant shopping mall. And somehow, we wait for three minutes at the post office and we're agitated because of the delay.

We've all heard the line: "Well, I wished for patience and look what happened!" The inference is that lots of longsuffering problems ensued. God's timing is different than ours. Take time with others, slow down, and look around you, meditate on God's Word. Your heart will listen better, your attitude will improve, and your problems will not deter you from happiness.

Is your life hectic? Can you think of ways or times you can pause and slow your heart and soul? Do you think you could benefit from this?

Sing of Strength

As for me, I shall sing of your strength;
Yes, I shall joyfully sing of your lovingkindness in the morning,
for you have been my stronghold
and a refuge in the day of my distress.

PSALM 59:16 NASB

We know the goodness of God personally because of the things which we have faced. In the midst of our distress, God remains our constant refuge and strength. If we focus on him rather than our hardships, we will clearly see that he is there with us through it all, not allowing us to fall, showing us the path to redemption.

God will not allow us to undergo more than we are capable of handling, but we were not meant to handle it alone. He is with us, so we cannot fail. If our burdens seem too big to carry, it could be that we are attempting to use our own strength rather than running to God.

How is a having a loving relationship with God a refuge?

Attention Please

> He who planted the ear, does he not hear?
> He who formed the eye, does he not see?
> PSALM 94:9 ESV

We live in a plugged-in society. Walk into any waiting room, and what do you see? Stand in most any line and people are doing the same thing. Try talking to a teenager in the car, or a family member sitting on the couch, and you will soon discover there is a lengthy distance from planet earth to the attention of another person. As much as technology makes up the working world, we still seek a mindless task to unwind. We plug in again. Here comes a clearing of the throat and a drumroll. Can God have our attention, please?

God is attentive. He made our ears and eyes. How ridiculous to entertain the thought that he doesn't see or hear what we do or say. He is an interactive God. He speaks to us through his Word, his Spirit and his Church. He relates to us. He wants relationship. Time unplugged allows us to listen, relate, and think. Our brains need pauses to ponder and reflect during the day. We benefit from waiting without distraction. As you wind down for the day, set aside distractions. Give God the quiet of your mind. Stop and listen. It may be that he is asking, "Can I have your attention, please?"

In what way does technology affect your attention to God?

Shout for Joy

May we shout for joy when we hear of your victory
and raise a victory banner in the name of our God.
May the LORD answer all your prayers.

PSALM 20:5 NLT

We often pray without expecting much of a response, so it is good to acknowledge those times when we see that God has answered our prayers. These stories in Scripture help to build our faith and so do the stories of our answered prayers. They are there to be shared.

Be encouraged today to continue to present your requests to God, knowing that he is listening. Even though you may have prayers and petitions that have not been answered yet, you know that sometimes the answer is different than what you were expecting. Continue to remember and share stories of the times when God has answered your prayers—shout for joy for all to hear!

What prayers has God answered for you lately?
Have you shared those stories with others yet?

With Passion

Listen to me all you godly ones: Love the Lord with passion!
The Lord protects and preserves all those who are loyal to him.
But he pays back in full all those who reject him in their pride.

PSALM 31:23 TPT

We put our heart and soul into the people, jobs, or hobbies that we are most excited about—the ones we love the most. They fuel us in a way that gives us energy. They motivate and inspire us to be our best. These passions can be our report card, giving us praise or critique depending on how we're doing.

It is with this very same passion that we should love, praise, and serve the Lord! Our greatest efforts should go toward our relationship with Jesus, the one who freed us from our bondage, and deeply pursues our heart.

*Can you put your effort toward your relationship with God?
He deserves all your praise, time, and energy. You are your best
self when you are in relationship with him. He will help
guide your passion by his Spirit.*

Feathers and Wings

His massive arms are wrapped around you, protecting you.
You can run under his covering of majesty and hide.
His arms of faithfulness are a shield keeping you from harm.
PSALM 91:4 TPT

We want to run and hide from many things in life, thinking that if we can run, difficulty will surely be gone when we choose to come back. We run because of fear. We run because of anger. We run because of indifference. We run, hoping someone will chase us. Hoping someone will come and find us.

God knows. He knows you. You matter to him. You mean something to the Creator of your life. He is not beyond whatever you are facing today. He tells you to run to him and he promises shelter and protection. He promises you that he will meet you in that place and give you peace. Run to him.

How has God been a shelter from all the things of this world
that make you afraid?

Not Our Power

We have this treasure in jars of clay to show that this all-surpassing power is from God and not from us.

2 CORINTHIANS 4:7 NIV

We've all heard a story: a 110-pound mother stops a moving car with her bare hands, or defeats a charging bear, to save her toddler. We love the image of the tiny defeating the mighty. The sheer unlikeliness of it is what makes it so compelling; love will make the impossible, possible.

When we feel called to do something for God, our first instinct may be to list our shortcomings. We focus on our ability, our strength, forgetting the One who promises to equip us with all we need. We are like Esther, wondering, What if I fail? The fact we could easily fail is what makes it a great story.

Have you felt God prompting you to do something that seems impossible? What if all you had to do was agree to try? Maybe you dream of accomplishing something but don't believe you could. What if he gave you that dream, and he's just waiting for you to ask for his help?

Laying Down Dreams

"I know that you can do all things,
and that no purpose of yours can be thwarted."

JOB 42:2 NRSV

What a beautiful thing it is to be living in step with the purposes of God. And not just a god, but the Alpha and the Omega, the all-knowing, all-powerful, only true God of the universe. How can we know though, that our dreams and plans align with his purposes? When they seem to be thwarted at every turn, how can we know that we are aligned with our God who can do all things?

First, be in the Word. Learn to study it, don't depend only on what others tell you about it. Next, pray for wisdom, and take direction. If you want to be able to hear God's voice you must obey in the little things. Lastly, be willing to lay your dreams down if he asks you to. Labor over your dreams and goals in prayer, constantly laying them at his feet. When you've done these things and feel the peace of being aligned to his purposes, then you will see areas that he is asking you to take steps of faith in to complete these purposes.

Do any of these steps resonate with you as one you might need to take in a current dream or life choice?

Blessed with Peace

The LORD gives strength to his people;
the LORD blesses his people with peace.

PSALM 29:11 NIV

What are the most relaxed times of your day or week? Is it when you go for a walk, or sit on the porch in the evening? It could be that first waking moment of your day when everything is quiet and calm. Peace is a very big part of the story of relaxing, whether it is having a calm spirit, a still body, or a still mind. We crave those moments in our ever increasingly busy world.

Before you approach the busy times, ask the Lord for peace. The psalm here says that he gives strength and blesses with peace. Rely on that promise, drink it in, until you feel equipped for the day ahead.

Can you thank the Lord right now for this moment
to still your heart, mind, and body?
Accept the blessing of peace that he has promised.

Everything in Love

Do everything in love.

1 CORINTHIANS 16:14 NCV

What goes through your mind as you shop for groceries? How about during your workouts? While you read, or watch TV, do your thoughts turn to love? As you do dishes, is there love in the way you rinse a glass, or as you dry a pot?

First Corinthians contains the rather extraordinary command to do everything in love. Everything. What would that look like? How does one pick lovingly through packages of strawberries, searching for the reddest, juiciest ones? Is there a loving way to scrub the broiler pan? Perhaps not, but we most certainly can approach our daily lives in a state of love, filled with it, thereby assuring all we do will be done in love.

Rather than consider how to bring more love to your activities, pray today asking to be filled to the brim with love. From there, simply let it flow.

Walk Steady

*Direct my footsteps according to your word;
let no sin rule over me.*
PSALM 119:133 NIV

What is it about high heels? Every family album contains a photo of an adorable toddler attempting to walk in Mama's shoes, and every woman remembers her first wobbly attempt to appear graceful in that first pair of pumps. How did she make it look so easy, so elegant? Most of us also have a memory of a not-so-graceful stumble or even a twisted ankle; yet, somehow the stiletto retains its appeal. Who hasn't relied on the steady arm of an escort or companion in far more sensible footwear?

Walking with Jesus is a little like learning to walk in four-inch heels. Others make it look so easy, gliding along apparently sinless while we feel shaky and uncertain, prone to stumble at any moment. Will we take a wrong step? Fall flat on our faces? (Do anyone else's feet hurt?) Lean on the strong arm of the Savior; allow him to steady you and direct your steps.

In which aspect of your walk do you feel the most steady and certain? The least? Share your confidence and your concerns with the Savior, and invite him to lead you in both.

Impossible

Behold, I will do a new thing,
Now it shall spring forth;
Shall you not know it?
I will even make a road in the wilderness
And rivers in the desert.

ISAIAH 43:19 NKJV

What seems impossible to you today? What have you given up on, walked away from, and written off as absurd? What dreams have you let die simply because you felt they were unattainable? Maybe our dreams, though they seem far off, were placed in our hearts for a purpose. And maybe they won't look exactly the way we always thought they would, but maybe they'll still come true in a new way. Maybe the things that seem insurmountable to us will be easily overcome when we shift perspective and look at them differently.

You serve a God who is powerful enough to make a path appear right through an empty wilderness and create a stream of life-giving water in the midst of a desert. He is more than able to take even the most impossible of situations and provide clarity, direction, and the means to make it through.

*Can you trust God with your impossibilities
and rely on his strength for your weaknesses?*

Chosen and Called

Moses said to the Lord, "Please, Lord, I have never been a skilled speaker.
Even now, after talking to you, I cannot speak well.
I speak slowly and can't find the best words."

EXODUS 4:10 NCV

When God asks us to do something, our first instinct is often to look around at who we feel could do it better. We wonder why God didn't choose that person, who—in our eyes—is clearly more qualified than we are. God could have chosen anyone to be his mouthpiece and his leader for the incredible work he did with the Israelites. He picked Moses. He knew what Moses' strengths and weaknesses were before he called him. And he still picked Moses.

Do you ever feel like God shouldn't have picked you for something? Do you think it would have been smarter for him to pick someone who is more creative, more intelligent, or more eloquent? You may not understand why God picked you for a certain task, but you can trust that when he calls you to do something, it's because he knows that you are not only capable, you are the one he wants to do the job.

*Why do you sometimes struggle to believe
that God has chosen you for something special?*

He Forgives

Keep me from the sins of pride;
don't let them rule me.
Then I can be pure and innocent
of the greatest of sins.

PSALM 19:13 NCV

When Jesus hung on the cross, there were two thieves hanging beside him. One of those thieves, as he hung in his final moments of life, asked Jesus for grace and a second chance. That thief—minutes before death—was given forgiveness and eternal life. The very same day he entered paradise as a forgiven and clean man.

In light of his story, how can we ever say that it's too late to turn it all around? Remember that God's mercy and forgiveness awaits each of us every single morning.

*Can you trust in that forgiveness today
and ask for a renewed sense of purpose?*

Image of Christ

*We all, who with unveiled faces contemplate the Lord's glory,
are being transformed into his image with ever-increasing glory,
which comes from the Lord, who is the Spirit.*

2 CORINTHIANS 3:18 NIV

When Moses witnessed the Lord, his face shone with a brightness
so pure it was unbearable to the other Israelites who had become
hardened in their sin. Similarly, the Lord intends for us to be his
reflection to the world. Light uncovers dark places and is often
uncomfortable to people who want to hide.

The Lord searches for every hidden heart, and he has chosen to use
us by shining through us. The way in which we behold God's glory
is not through good works or study but when God removes the veil
separating us and shines his face upon us.

How do you see God's light shining in and through you?

Trustworthiness

A gossip betrays a confidence;
so avoid anyone who talks too much.
PROVERBS 20:19 NIV

When someone confides in us, to break that confidence is a breach of trust. There are always exceptions when safety is in question, but if the motive of our hearts is self-centered, it is a telling sign that we should remain quiet. The secrets of others are never meant as a tool to further our own reputations.

Our character before the Lord should matter to us far more than our standings with others. We ought to strive to be people of trustworthiness and discretion. Others should feel safe and cared for when they willingly share their hearts with us.

*Would you consider yourself trustworthy
with information told to you in confidence?*

Weight of Grace

Then Cain said to the LORD, "This punishment is more than I can stand! Today you have forced me to stop working the ground, and now I must hide from you. I must wander around on the earth, and anyone who meets me can kill me." The LORD said to Cain, "No! If anyone kills you, I will punish that person seven times more." Then the Lord put a mark on Cain warning anyone who met him not to kill him.

GENESIS 4:13-15 NCV

When the news flashes the story of a man who killed another man in cold blood, our hearts rise up within us. We become angry, almost plagued, by the injustice of what we are hearing. We wait to hear the punishment. What if the judge laid down his gavel and announced that the murderer would not be condemned, and he would be protected by the court? That wouldn't seem quite fair, would it?

Cain offered an unacceptable sacrifice to God, murdered his innocent brother on account of jealousy, and lied about his brother's death. Though God was grieved by Cain's sin, he showed him remarkable grace—grace in the form of an indelible mark of protection. This is the weight of grace: a grace so vast, so encompassing that even the most dreadful murderer is covered by the love and mercy of God. And it's yours today.

Can you accept the mercy of God today?

Rewards of Fellowship

"Where two or three are gathered together in my name,
I am there in the midst of them."

MATTHEW 18:20 NKJV

When was the last time you felt spiritually recharged from conversation or prayer with other Christians? Sometimes going to church, a woman's group, or a Bible study seems like just another thing to add to your list of things to do.

God is a relational God. He knows that we need each other, and that life is better together. As a Christian, it is especially important to share time with other believers. When we make time to pray together, study the Bible together, and share our faith stories, we can be supported, encouraged, and strengthened.

Are you giving yourself an opportunity to be uplifted by other believers or to be an encouragement to those around you? Remember that God promises to be with you when you are gathered together in his name. Actively seek his presence with others, and experience the rich rewards of fellowship.

Surefooted and Strong

He makes me as surefooted as a deer,
enabling me to stand on mountain heights.

PSALM 18:33 NLT

When we are walking God's way, we can be as surefooted as a deer because we will not question the integrity of our steps. Even on a high mountain, we do not need to fear because we know that the Lord is guiding us.

God has trained our hands and our feet to operate according to his will, and so whatever comes our way we know that we have the strength to face it. He is the skip in our step. We can be confident because he is our diligent guide and we experience so much joy when we follow him. He makes us surefoooted and strong, capable of facing anything that tries to distract us from pursuing him.

*Does walking in God's perfect way mean you will not
face trouble? Why does God give you strength
and train your hands for battle?*

The Table

The Christmas season is like no other. You're invited to Christmas parties where you get to dress up and make your favorite appetizer. You can snuggle up on the couch and drink hot chocolate while watching old classics as your Christmas tree lights twinkle behind you. You can get together with girlfriends who are in different stages of life and have a memorable night of laughter and fun. The season feels almost magical.

One of the best areas to experience this time of year is around the table. Something beautiful happens when friends and family gather around delicious food. Conversation can lead almost anywhere. The beauty of the Christmas season is discovered in smiles, laughter, and joy-filled memories.

In this season, is there a time you can gather loved ones together and have a laughter-filled evening?

Great News

"Today in the town of David a Savior has been born to you;
he is the Messiah, the Lord."

LUKE 2:11 NIV

When heaven touches earth, something is going to change. Shepherds in the field witnessed angels descending, and they fell into great fear. Why? Because we are not holy and worthy, by our own accord, to witness or stand in the presence of the Holy One. We are not sinless, and something within us knows we have no right to stand before the perfectly holy.

The angels adjured the shepherds to be fearless. They had great news that would give joy to the whole world. Jesus, God and man, the only sinless one, would make us holy so we could stand before God and feel the utter joy of his presence. What a relief! We no longer have to stand in fear because Jesus has eradicated the need for shame.

*How can you reach out to others with the favor, love,
and grace that Jesus has given you?*

Joy to the World

Let the sea and everything in it shout his praise!
Let the earth and all living things join in.
PSALM 98:7 NLT

Joy to the world, the Lord has come! When Christ came as a little child, he not only brought joy to the people of the day that knew he was the Savior, he also brought joy to the entire world.

We celebrate because we know the significance of Christ being born as a human, entering in to our existence, and displaying what it meant to be fully alive. The restoration that Christ brings is something that will extend to all living things, and this is why can have joy on this day—we know that there is hope for the whole created world. Celebrate this hope as you celebrate this day.

How can you express joy today as you celebrate Christ's birth?

The Voice of Love

"The Father gives me the people who are mine.
Every one of them will come to me,
and I will always accept them."
JOHN 6:37 NCV

When we live for other voices, we will quickly become worn out and discouraged. Other people's expectations for how we should live, act, and be are sometimes unreachable. There is one voice that matters, and it can come in a variety of forms—the voice of God.

What God would tell us is that we are loved, we are cherished, and we have significant value. We are his beloved, his daughters, his beautiful creation. This is the voice that matters. This is the voice to come back to when we feel like we're not enough.

What are the voices you typically listen to? Can you ignore them and focus only on the voice that matters? He will encourage you and remind you that you are enough. Nothing you do or don't do is going to make him love you any more or any less. Soak it in, so you can drown out all the other voices.

Encouragement

Worry weighs a person down;
an encouraging word cheers a person up.
PROVERBS 12:25 NLT

When worry overtakes us, being reminded of the truth can offer great reprieve. A true friend provides encouragement and cheer, helping the worried to lift their burdens. Worry is like a weight that pulls us down. It imagines the possible negative outcomes and fixates on failures. Worry forgets the Lord's faithfulness and forgoes his help.

By simply offering an encouraging word, we have the power to reassure others and restore their hope. It may not seem like words carry much weight, but they have the power to break someone down or build them up. We should strive to be responsible and loving in the way we use our words.

How do you know what to say to someone in their worry?
What is an example of an encouraging word?

Sideline

The LORD of Heaven's Armies is here among us;
the God of Israel is our fortress.

PSALM 46:7 NLT

When you are watching your favorite sports team play, you remain completely invested in what is happening with each player and move. Everyone on the other team, whether player or spectator, feels like the enemy. It's good to be part of a team and to cheer people on even when you are on the sideline.

The next time you feel like someone in your community, friendship circle, or family is starting to have a difficult time, make sure that you spend some time investing in cheering them on and encouraging them to pick themselves up and keep going.

*How can you encourage someone in your community
with words or actions today?*

Spiritual Gifts

As each has received a gift,
use it to serve one another,
as good stewards of God's varied grace.

1 PETER 4:10 ESV

When you see an orchestra perform, you will notice there are a variety of instruments. Violins strumming softly. Horn instruments all ready to explode with triumph. Flutes and clarinets that steadily lead you along, percussion that can be as subtle as a triangle or as monumental as the cymbals crashing. In the same way, we have each been given various gifts. Your gifting will not be the same or play out in the same way as others'. Just as the instruments are all varied, so can be the music they play.

You can't be ashamed of the boldness your cymbal crashing may entail, or the quiet significance your steady rhythm drum brings. Each of us have a gift to use that we cannot waste our time wondering if those around us think our gift is worthy, fitting, or significant. Use your gift to join in harmony with the music being played to the glory of God by the body of Christ. Every crash, every soft verse, every rise and fall of a string has its place. Serve God boldly in your gifts today.

In what way can you uncover your gift and use it to its fullest?

Preserved with Integrity

Let integrity and uprightness preserve me,
for I wait for You.
PSALM 25:21 NASB

When you think of great leaders who have stood the test of time, what is it that really defines them? A good leader has integrity. They can withstand all kinds of difficulties because in the midst of them they are preserved by the very fact that they cannot be faulted by immorality or injustice. We might not like some of the characteristics or personality traits of certain leaders, but if they have proven time and time again to be people of their word, they will continue to flourish.

This Scripture attests to the principle that being a person of integrity will preserve your life and keep you from all kinds of accusations. If you are tempted to stray today, remember to wait for the Lord to rescue you.

*Who can you thank in your life for
modeling the character of integrity?*

Unqualified

Though a mighty army surrounds me,
my heart will not be afraid.
Even if I am attacked,
I will remain confident.
PSALM 27:3 NLT

Whether bringing a brand new baby home from the hospital, giving your first major presentation at work, or making your first big meal for guests, there's probably been at least one moment in your life that had you thinking, *I have no idea what I'm doing. I'm not qualified.*

What did you do? You probably had little option but to dive on in! Let your confidence in God's ability be the driver today. You will feel a lot calmer when you realize this day does not have to be done in your own strength. The Lord is the one who hands out qualifications and all you need to do is ask for his help.

As you move into a new year, how can you determine to ask God for help and remember that you are not alone?